T0381468

AN 80-YEAR JOURNEY

(1945-2025,
AND COUNTING)

ALAN H. GOODMAN

authorHOUSE®

AuthorHouse™
1663 Liberty Drive
Bloomington, IN 47403
www.authorhouse.com
Phone: 833-262-8899

Published by AuthorHouse 10/31/2024

ISBN: 979-8-8230-3656-6 (sc)
ISBN: 979-8-8230-3657-3 (e)

Library of Congress Control Number: 2024922595

Print information available on the last page.

CONTENTS

Book 1 Introduction 1

    1945 3

    1963 4

    Adjusting to Old Age 5

    Stress and Anxiety 6

Book 2 Hurricane Katrina – Rebuilding Our Lives 8

    Hurricane Katrina 8

    Other Things Related to Katrina 29

    Some Final Thoughts about Katrina 33

Book 3 The Importance of Stress, Routines, Games, Friends, Judaism, Christmas, and Raising Children 38

    My Current Stress 38

    Routine 39

    Games 40

    Friends 41

    My Children 42

    Judaism 43

    Christmas 45

    Raising Children 47

    The American Dream? 49

Book 4 Journey of Alan 50

    The Early Years: Up to Age 14 50

    The Magical Years: Ages 15-17 53

    The Come Down Years: Ages 18-22 65

    The Law School and Vietnam War Years –

    Lots of Drama: Ages 22-25 70

    The Good Years – Getting Married: Ages 26-30 78

    The Better Years – Returning to New

    Orleans and Children: Ages 30-40 88

    The Even Better Years – And More

    Children: Ages 40-49 96

    The Good Years Continue: Ages 50-59 121

    Katrina and The Law Practice: Age 60-69 126

    All Good Years Too: Ages 70-79 130

Conclusion 137

....

BOOK ONE

INTRODUCTION

I always admired and looked up to scholar-athletes. Many in our society did too. That doesn't seem to be the case nowadays, in 2024, and the scholar-athlete seems to be a relic of the past. My story is one of a scholar-athlete.

I graduated as the Second Honor Student in my high school, Isidore Newman School ("Newman"), which is considered the best academically in New Orleans. I have always enjoyed learning. The learning process is work, laborious at times, but it feels good when I've learned things.

I was also the football quarterback for one undefeated year, something the school had never achieved and still hasn't, and was an All-State guard in basketball on two undefeated teams, something else the school had never achieved and still hasn't. Newman is the high school of some great professional athletes like Peyton Manning, Eli Manning, Odell Beckham, Jr., and Randy Livingston (who now coaches basketball at Newman). Our only coach in football and basketball who was then just 29 years old was Edward "Skeets" Tuohy.

In his first year at Newman (my sophomore year), Coach Tuohy led the school to 8-0 in football and 32-0 in basketball, the only sports in which Newman competed against other schools. He removed a sign in our gym that said "It's not whether you win or lose, it's how you play the game." He thought that was a crock of bullshit, and he was right that the only thing that mattered was whether the team won. Did I love that he did that? Yep!

During his first year we posted a large banner across the back wall of the gym saying "Welcome to Death Valley." We never lost a home game during my three years of playing varsity basketball.

Coach Tuohy was beyond intense. He hated to lose. Don't we all? He yelled at us; he even smacked some of us; he was extremely animated on the sidelines during games; and we won. I became extremely intense during those three years of high school, perhaps emulating Coach Tuohy, and continued afterwards to be just as intense in my life. Indeed, my intensity would sometimes boil over into anger – which was never directed at my teammates – and even extreme anger when we were losing in games, and that extreme anger/ intensity helped me to find ways to win in sports and in life.

I also laugh a lot, which is good for my soul, and enjoy life for the most part. As my brother Malcolm lovingly described me in a poem for my wedding:

> "Alan, Alan Goodman,
> The glad lad with the giggly laugh,
> The mild child with a smile and a half."

Coach Tuohy also laughed and enjoyed life, or so it always seemed. Indeed, one of Coach Tuohy's children is Sean Tuohy whose family was featured in the book "The Blind Side" by Michael Lewis (Sean and Michael were both Newman graduates too) which later became a hit movie.

I have always valued my family – both as a son and as a husband-father – as well as hard work in my endeavors, whatever they were at the time. I have enjoyed being important through my achievements in school, work, and family. Don't most people strive for these things?

This book is my "legacy will" to my four children and their families, including their spouses, children, grandchildren, great grandchildren, and so on forever. I would have loved if my father or mother had written a "legacy will" about their lives and ancestors, and this is my story and my gift.

1945

1945 was a momentous year in American history. World War II ended; the horrors of the Holocaust were uncovered and broadcast; and I was born.

Just 80 years earlier in 1865, the Civil War ended. Think about that for a moment – just 80 years prior to my being, our country fought a Civil War over slavery. I'm proud to be an American but I'm not proud over that part of our history. As I would learn later first-hand, the Germans are likewise not proud of their history regarding World War II and the Holocaust. But, I do not blame the Germans for the sins of their parents, just as I do not blame Americans for the sins of our forefathers.

Something else worth pondering is that 80 years prior to the end of the Civil War, or in 1785, this Country was being formed through the Declaration of Independence, the Revolutionary War, and the signing of the U.S. Constitution. It would seem that about every 80 years this Country goes through highly momentous events. What awaits us in 2025?

I am the third of three boys. My Dad lived until he was 99. My Mother died of Alzheimer's at age 79 (my age now). As I tell my family, if I don't lose my mind, I should live well into my 90's or beyond.

We are Jewish, which is something I never considered important until I did in my twenties.

I love the meritocracy of the United States and learned to thrive in it. While the upward mobility in this Country may not be as attainable in 2024, it was good during my formative years and I took full advantage of the opportunities that came my way. As the saying goes, "the great football teams make their own breaks, and are not lucky." While I no doubt enjoyed certain advantages in life, I believe in my heart that I capitalized on mine to the utmost and earned my success through hard work.

1963 was the height of my life up until then. What fun being the Captain of the football and basketball teams and going 32-0 in basketball for the second time. What a high!

And then graduating as the Second Honor Student.

I'm 5 feet 7 ½ inches, which is short for basketball. I never allowed my lack of height or my being Jewish to deter me from succeeding.

1963

I was awarded and accepted a basketball scholarship to Tulane University which was then in the SEC. After Tulane I attended Georgetown Law School in Washington, D.C.; after law school I served as a law clerk for Judge Charles Fahy on the United States Court of Appeals for the D.C. Circuit for a year; and after my one-year clerkship I entered the real world at age 26 and accepted a position with Covington & Burling, the number one law firm in our Nation's Capital at the time and now.

The cultural revolution of the 1960's and early 1970's was in full-blown mode when I resided in D.C. The play "Hair," the rock opera "Jesus Christ Superstar," and the movie "Woodstock" (which was a large music festival) first appeared during this time. The Black People's March on Washington, D.C. occurred then too, along with Martin Luther King Jr.'s "I Have a Dream" speech. Marches in protest against the Vietnam War happened then too. Those were turbulent times in America.

This Country also landed a man on the moon for the first time ever.

I am proud to be part of that generation of America which changed it forever.

It was in 1971 while at Covington in D.C. that I met Sherrie. There was passion and fun from the outset; there was also something else that was important for my parents, and for me apparently. She is Jewish. We got engaged seven weeks after we met and then married five months later. The marriage has worked well for us, and we now have a large family of 19 which is still growing and includes our four children and their spouses and children.

In 1975 when Sherrie was pregnant with our first child, we decided to move back home to New Orleans. I was lucky to have a "cool" city where I grew up and to have a lot of family there. It has proven to be a good move for us.

Adjusting to Old Age

I can't tell you when I became old. It just creeps up on you until you realize you're old.

I'm age 79 (and thus in my 80th year of life) and am still a practicing attorney with a major law firm, which allows me to be with young, bright, energetic people every day, discussing weighty legal or practical issues, and to earn money. Paychecks are nice and appreciated.

On Monday mornings it "feels good" to be cleaned up again and to be at the office working and being social with others. I recall after Hurricane Katrina in 2005, when we had been displaced to Houston for four months, how I felt when I returned to New Orleans and sat behind my desk for the first time. It felt good.

Work is good for my soul, whatever and however one's soul is defined. It just "feels" good.

I learned about 50 years ago to recognize and trust my feelings, especially for the life-altering decisions one has to make from time to time. Books have been written on the subject. The lessons I've learned about decision-making are, first, trust your feelings (or "stomach") and, second, do not make a decision unless and until your feelings and your brain (or "head") are aligned that the decision is the correct one. It has taken me months at times to reach a decision. I've also been unable at times to have my feelings and brain aligned regarding major decisions. In those instances I continued with the status quo without making any change or decision.

This process has worked well for me.

Stress and Anxiety

I've also learned that a certain level of stress in life is healthy.

When I was in my late 30's and went on a nice, long, relaxing vacation, I came to realize during it that I missed the stress in my life. What I did was call one of my younger law partners (Bill) during the vacation regarding pending matters to give him tasks to do in them. That probably stressed him; he was probably enjoying my absence from the office. Years later Bill reminded me in a nice way that if I switched the consonants of my first name, Alan, the word became "anal." 😊 The incident of my calling Bill from vacation made me realize that I require stress in my life to be happy. Practicing law – a stressful occupation – suits me well.

When stress reaches anxiety, though, that's not a good thing. I've learned through the years that too much stress can cause anxiety, which can be exhibited in different ways, including stomach aches from acid and sleeplessness at night.

What I have learned to do at such times is to search my feelings to determine what is causing the anxiety and then to deal with the cause. I don't run from the problem. I deal with it, one baby step at a time, until the anxiety is lessened to stress.

Most of these times involved a difficult case. I would then dig even deeper into the matter, figure out the best course forward for the client (and me), and then carry out that plan. The results were almost always very good for the client and for me, just as in sports.

But not always. When things didn't work out so well for the client and for me, I managed that situation too. Losing is not fun at all, but I've learned not to despair over it and to move on to the next matter. After all, what other choice does one have. I asked a cousin once how he dealt with the loss of one of his children. His answer: What choice did he have other than to move ahead. His despair lessened over time.

BOOK TWO

HURRICANE KATRINA – REBUILDING OUR LIVES

Hurricane Katrina

Hurricane Katrina was the ultimate stress/anxiety event in my life. I was 60 at the time. Our home of over 25 years flooded badly. It was effectively destroyed. We were homeless for four months. Think about that for a moment as if it could happen to you one day. Think about it again and again.

We had two teenagers at the time and our two older children, Tiffany and Allison, were out of the house with their own adult soul mates. Dustin, our 14-year old, was in 9th grade, and Brittany, our 13-year old, was in 8th grade. Those were tender and important years for them. Sherrie and I thus had them with us during these high stress times filled with anxiety.

We evacuated New Orleans early August 29, 2005 for our own safety and drove to Houston to stay with my brother Malcolm and his wife Connie. Evacuating the City is not a routine my parents ever practiced, even though back then there were no levees to prevent flooding of the City from Lake Pontchartrain. And there were some very bad hurricanes back then that wacked New Orleans, including (just as one example) Hurricane Betsy in the 1960's which caused severe flooding in the eastern parts of New Orleans when certain canals flowing from the Lake into the City overflowed into the City.

In 2005 there were levees at the Lake and along the canals in New Orleans to prevent flooding from ever occurring again. Who worried about flooding? I certainly didn't. Yet, Hurricane Katrina was the largest hurricane ever, a category 5 (the highest), and it was headed right at us. Sherrie and I both felt that with two teenagers in the house we should drive over to Houston for a day or two and then could return home if the damages from the high winds weren't bad. I packed lightly – a few pairs of shorts, shirts, etc., some cash, and no checkbook.

The year before Katrina, in 2004, there was another large hurricane threatening the City but we didn't evacuate for it because it turned to the East of us a day before it hit land.

In 2005 our evacuation to Houston took 15-16 hours, which is normally a 5 ½ hour drive. That drive was miserable: We would creep along I-10 at 10-15 miles per hour for long stretches of time; at one point when an ambulance pulled onto the shoulder blaring its siren, I pulled behind it and said "lead the way Mother Fucker;" but then the ambulance exited after a few miles. During the drive's later stages I announced to Sherrie and the kids that I would never evacuate again (my parents never did, which worked out well for them, and we had never either before Katrina) if this was a false alarm. Saying that may not have been one of my finer moments.

I recall watching the national news on television after August 29, 2005 and seeing images of the interstate highway flooded and then our own neighborhood badly flooded too. That's when I realized how bad things were going to be for us. The levees had failed and collapsed. We were homeless for the first time ever. I called Sherrie who was out shopping with the children and asked her to come home right away.

Some questions at the time were: Would New Orleans

ever be revived as a city? Where should we plan to live for the rest of our lives? What should I do at age 60? What should we do for the rest of our lives?

But those were long-term issues for which there were no answers.

Over the first few days we realized that we had to address our very near-term needs first, such as cash, cell phones (which were not as common then), and clothes. After figuring out where I banked in New Orleans and whether Houston had a branch of it (it did), I went there and explained our situation. The bank was accommodating after verifying everything about us, and I obtained $1,000 in cash and some checks.

Check off cash. √ Phew!!

Next we decided to go to Austin, which is about three hours from Houston, to visit Tiffany (our oldest) and her family for the Labor Day weekend. Allison, our second child, evacuated there with her fiancé (Mario), and we wanted to be with them that first weekend, figuring it may be many months before we would see them again. It was good to be together, all six of us, which we now call "Yo Fam."

Allison was scheduled to be married that December in New Orleans. We discussed her possibly getting married in Austin in early September at Tiffany's house with just us and a few others in attendance. She said no, because she wanted to be married in New Orleans where they lived too. I told her a wedding in December in New Orleans was impossible given the sorry state of the City. She understood and was okay delaying the wedding until the Spring when possibly the City would be inhabitable again.

That weekend in Austin we went to some outlets about 45 minutes outside of Austin to shop for clothes. I bought clothes that I would be wearing for the foreseeable future (say 3-4 months) and were suitable for work and weekends. We also bought clothes for Sherrie and the kids, Dustin and Brittany.

Check off clothes. √ Phew!!

We still had to get cell phones. We did that too.

Check off cell phones. √ Phew!!

After that Labor Day weekend in Austin we returned to Houston. Next on our list of things to do, in no particular order, were figuring out (a) school for the kids which had just started, (b) where to live for the next few months, if not longer, and (c) how to deal with my law firm and law practice.

By that next weekend we managed to get Dustin and Brittany into a good school in Houston. Their New Orleans school, Newman (yes, the same one I attended), told everyone that it would be shut down until at least January. Newman is a private school, and the three best private schools in Houston agreed to accept the Newman students who had evacuated to Houston. Since my brother Malcolm and his wife Connie knew about the Houston schools, their advice was helpful. I had two good friends from my Tulane University days (David and Jack) who were living in Houston at the time, and we obtained their input too. Kincaid School turned out to be our preference, and Dustin and Brittany were accepted to Kincaid.

I was expecting to be required to pay tuition to Kincaid for that semester, if not the year. It turns out that Kincaid adopted a new policy, just for Katrina evacuees attending it, that (a) you were welcome to stay until your New Orleans school reopened (if ever), (b) as long as you paid your New Orleans school the tuition due it (which we had paid for the first semester), you were not required to pay any tuition to Kincaid, and (c) once your New Orleans school reopened, you were no longer welcome at Kincaid as a show of support for the New Orleans schools. How nice was that for Kincaid to do!

Check off schooling for Dustin and Brittany. √ Phew!!

They liked Kincaid and made new friends there. Kincaid was not as difficult for them academically as was Newman. When we later learned that Newman would reopen in January for the second semester, we all wanted to move back to New Orleans to live. As nice as everyone in Houston was to us, it just was not home for us.

Next on our to do list was where to live for the foreseeable future. The choice of Kincaid decided that for us: Houston it would be. We also considered relocating to Baton Rouge (where my firm had an office) or Shreveport (where my firm also had an office), but we learned that the better schools in both cities were quickly running out of spaces, that housing in Baton Rouge was becoming impossible to find, and that we were better off in the big city of Houston which was better able to accommodate the evacuees and where we had found a good school for the kids.

Next on our list was my work and where to live in Houston. After two weeks of being in Houston and staying with Malcolm and Connie, we decided that we wanted our own space for living. We also decided that Sherrie would begin to look for a place for us to live, and I would commute to Shreveport for the week for my work.

I rented a car for a week; drove to Shreveport (about a 4-hour drive) early Monday for the week; stayed with my brother Carl and his wife Sylvia while there; and went to work in our Shreveport office. Although I was Vice-Chairman of the firm, I was given a small interior office (no windows) for work and got busy practicing law. It felt good to be in an office again and to be practicing law again. I got my first laptop computer ever and learned how to use it. I started calling clients to check in with them. Everyone was relieved to hear from me and learn I was alive and well.

A few weeks after Katrina -- after the water in the City had been pumped back into Lake Pontchartrain – a group of our attorneys rented a large truck to retrieve client files from our New Orleans office which we needed for our law practice along with such things as our work calendars and rolodexes (with clients' names and contact information) and other needed stuff. This was before the age of personal laptops for all attorneys which now perform these functions. They brought beers with them to give to the officers when they were stopped outside the City in order to help persuade the officers to allow them entry into the City. In the early weeks after Katrina it was hard to get into the City and there were National Guard officers controlling who could enter for legitimate reasons.

This routine – going to Shreveport early Mondays, working there for the week, and returning to Houston late Fridays – continued for about six weeks. I compared the weekends in Houston to conjugal visits for prisoners – a bad joke of course – and it was good to be with my own family for the weekends. Sherrie felt like the wife in the play/movie "Fiddler on the Roof" (after we rented a townhouse) when she would clean the house and prepare dinner for Friday when I returned, which is the start of the Jewish Sabbath (which goes from sunset Friday to sunset Saturday). We would celebrate the Sabbath (and being together) by lighting two Sabbath candles while reciting a prayer in Hebrew; then bless the wine with another Hebrew prayer; and then slice the Challah (a Jewish bread) with another Hebrew prayer. Again, it was good to be together.

All of the courts in New Orleans were closed, and so in litigation work (which most of us did) there were no courts for a couple of months, but there was still pre-trial work to do. Working during this period of time was challenging, but it was important for all of us and for our clients. Again, it felt good to be back at work.

Through August of 2005, our firm was having a very good year. We decided three important things quickly: (1) We would not lay off or reduce the compensation of any of our associates (attorneys) and staff (non-attorneys) and would continue to pay them; (2) we would continue to pay all partners their monthly draws; and (3) we would make a substantial distribution to the partners to help during these difficult times. This made us all appreciate the law firm.

Check off work. √ Phew!!

That Friday when I returned to Houston for the weekend, I decided that I needed my own car and bought one that weekend. It was not economical for me to rent a car weekly. I had learned that my car, which we left in New Orleans, flooded badly and was ruined, and I now needed my own car. Rather than pay cash for it (which was my practice) I leased it for four years, which is really the same as financing a new car but is less expensive because after four years I had to return it. I was relieved to have my own wheels, and Sherrie still used the Ford Expedition we drove to evacuate New Orleans.

Check off a car for me. √ Phew!!

Sherrie continued to look for a place for us to live in Houston. She was not having much luck. Landlords wanted leases of at least a year, and rents were high. It was the next week when she finally found a 3-bedroom townhouse for us to rent. I had looked at it and a few other places over the weekend. The landlord insisted on a lease of no fewer than six months and was charging a premium rent for the shorter term. Sherrie called me in Shreveport for help and told me the situation. By this time, we were beginning to hope that New

Orleans would be able to reopen by Christmas. Figuring there is a price for everything, I asked Sherrie to call the landlord and offer him the following: (a) A lease of four months ending December 31, 2005; (b) a higher rent to be decided by him for the shorter term; and (c) prepayment of all four months of rent. Surprisingly, the landlord quoted a monthly rent that was not much higher but wanted a certified or cashier's check for the rent prepayment. We agreed and had our own place for that next weekend.

Check off a place to live until Christmas. √ Phew!!

The townhouse was not furnished. Rental furniture in Houston was no longer available due to the many evacuees there. In two days that weekend, we managed to buy inexpensive furniture from two stores, including furniture for the three bedrooms we had, the dining area, the den area, and the kitchen which entailed plates, glasses, utensils, pots and pans, and other such things like pillows, sheets, towels, etc. That was a harrowing weekend, because the reality had settled in that most of our beautiful furnishings in New Orleans which we had accumulated over three decades were destroyed by Katrina.

Check off furniture. √ Phew!!

Regarding my work, I continued the routine of leaving early Mondays and returning late Fridays. For six weeks that meant going to Shreveport and back. Our office in New Orleans reopened in mid-October, and starting then until Christmas I drove to New Orleans and back.

It felt especially good to get back into my own office in New Orleans with access to my secretary and other attorneys who returned there to work.

While in New Orleans I stayed in my wife's sister's (Sue's) empty and undamaged home in Metairie, an adjoining neighborhood in Jefferson Parish (same as a county elsewhere).

Sue and her husband Freddie were in Baton Rouge at the time. They had bought a house there to accommodate their children and Sue's and Sherrie's parents (who were not in good health) to reside.

New Orleans as a City had not yet returned to any semblance of normal by mid-October, nor had Metairie which had not flooded (except for parts). When I traveled early Mondays to New Orleans I had to bring not only clothes for the week but also food and water (and wine). It was surreal being in New Orleans. It felt like I was in a war zone: Almost nothing was open, including stores and gas stations; there were very few people in the City; the tap water was not drinkable; and driving among the ruins of the City was very upsetting and almost depressing. That continued for two months until Christmas.

Check off being able to work in New Orleans again. √ Phew!!

We still had to deal with a place to live in New Orleans when we returned as well as our flooded home.

Our home in New Orleans was two stories with the bedrooms upstairs. We had built a swimming pool in the backyard, and we had two beautiful Magnolia trees in the front of the house. Our home took on 8 ½ feet of water. The downstairs, which we had furnished beautifully, was destroyed, and there was very little we could salvage. Our cousin had gone into the house and sent us pictures. We knew how bad it was beforehand. Allison (our daughter) had gone there too and warned us it was really bad. But it was much worse in real life than we had imagined, as we discovered when we first set foot in it.

In October, still just weeks after Katrina, we decided our next task was to deal with our New Orleans home. We rented a small trailer to hook onto our Ford Expedition and drove to

New Orleans for a few days. We left Dustin and Brittany to stay with their new friends in Houston. We also managed to locate movers in Baton Rouge who met us at our New Orleans home, and we rented a large storage unit in New Orleans for any salvageable furniture. Just being able to find movers and a storage unit were small miracles at the time. Sherrie had heard from friends that it was risky to go into our home due to mold and diseases, and so she bought Hazmat suits for us. It was still very hot in New Orleans.

We went to our destroyed home early the next morning, donned our Hazmat suits, and entered the house for the first time. That day was traumatic. The front doors were unlocked and open, because all the water in the house blew them open so the water could escape. Much of the furniture throughout the downstairs had drifted to the foyer of the house. Our pink Baby Grand Piano in the living room was turned upside down as it floated in the water. We saw the water line 8 ½ feet above the floors.

We walked through the downstairs to assess everything. It was awful. The kitchen was the worst. We did not open the refrigerator and freezer doors because we had been told that all the food would be badly spoiled and the odor would be overwhelming.

We next walked upstairs in what was left of the stairway. I went first, and very slowly, in case the steps had rotted and in case the whole stairway might collapse. It didn't and Sherrie followed. We quickly discovered that we also had roof damage due to Katrina, and there was mold on the upstairs walls. The mattresses were mildewed and we left them. But some of the bedroom furniture upstairs was salvageable.

Basically, some of the upstairs (including most of our clothes) was okay along with a few items downstairs.

Sherrie wanted to salvage our good China and silverware,

which was in a low cabinet across the dining room. When I opened the cabinet doors water poured out. This was not rainwater. It was nasty salt water from the Lake which no doubt was badly polluted. I recall kneeling down to remove the China and silverware very carefully and bringing it outside. That was not enjoyable.

The movers arrived a few hours later. We told them what to remove from our home and put into their truck. We put our clothes and a few other things in the trailer that we had hooked onto Sherrie's Expedition to bring back to Houston. Afterwards the movers met us at the storage unit we had rented in the City to unload their truck into it.

When we left the house Sherrie recited the Kaddish, which is the Hebrew prayer for the dead. What that meant for us was that we were saying goodbye to our dream home: The large house that we could barely afford to buy 26 years earlier; the house that we furnished so beautifully and enjoyed immensely; the house where we raised our four children; the house that brought so much joy and pride for Sherrie and me and our children. That was a sad day for us.

In terms of housing in New Orleans for us when we returned, the economical thing for us would have been to rebuild our home. The structure was still seemingly good and rebuilding it would have been less expensive than buying a new home in the City, of which there were not many that had not flooded. But then and there, Sherrie and I both felt that we did not want to do that, because we would have just compared any rebuilt home to what we had previously and it never would have been the same for us. We also had two sick parents (Sherrie's) and two active teenagers; finding contractors and materials was difficult; and we would not have had the time to rebuild our home.

Check off, in part, dealing with our ruined home and our furniture and clothes from it. √ Phew!!

We still needed somewhere to live in New Orleans when we returned for Christmas. That next day while in New Orleans we started looking. Initially, we thought we might be able to find something to rent for six months while we looked for our next home. We were unable to find anything which was suitable for us, and rental properties which had not flooded were scarce.

We also still needed to deal with our ruined home. What our friends and others we knew were doing, and suggested we should do, was to hire a contractor to gut the house to its wooden studs and brick exterior, and after that try to sell it for whatever we could get.

Since I was in New Orleans weekly, I undertook those tasks while Sherrie dealt with the kids and our townhouse in Houston.

I found a reputable contractor through a law partner who was reasonably priced and hired him. When his work was completed after two days, I went to inspect the house, and what I found was this: Two mountains about 25 feet high each of trash and debris on the front lawn, which the City (or FEMA) would pick up and remove in the coming weeks; the downstairs was gutted to the concrete foundation and the wood frames; all the floors were ruined, except for the marble floor in the front of the house and the brick floor in the den; there were no walls, except the brick walls from the outside and the black sheetrock which held the brick from the inside; and there were no ceilings, except light bulbs and wires hanging from the ceiling wooden frames. The wooden staircase was still there but was treacherous to climb. Upstairs was mostly intact, except there was mold on the walls and the carpeting was mildewed.

After the house was gutted, I posted a "For Sale" sign outside, and after about 2-3 months managed to sell it. The house pre-Katrina was worth over $1 million. We sold it for about $290,000.

Check off gutting and selling our house. √ Phew!!

We were still homeless in New Orleans, though. Basically, all of New Orleans (Orleans Parish) had flooded to a greater or lesser extent, except for what came to be known locally as the Sliver by the River or the Isle of Denial. The French who first settled New Orleans did so along the "high ground" close to the Mississippi River. The French Quarter in downtown New Orleans is close to the River and did not flood. Basically, the Sliver by the River was about 1 mile (or less) from the River and encompassed the parts of the City running along the winding River in the City. Lake Pontchartrain is about 8-9 miles north of the River, and the City became populated over time from the River to the Lake. Probably 80 percent of the City's homes had flooded. We did not want to live anywhere that had flooded and so were restricted in our search for a new home.

We realized soon that rental properties were scarce, expensive, and not very nice. I don't think I need to explain the difficulties generally in finding and buying a home, and just multiply that about 5 times. After about two months I found a townhouse to buy, which had three bedrooms (and a small fourth if needed), 3 ½ baths, and was located in the Sliver. Sherrie did not like it, though. After much discussion and some pressure from me – telling her that there was nothing else available within our price range, that we would still have to furnish any place we lived, and that we could still look for another home while there – she relented and we bought it. I liked it. It was large enough for us to live comfortably and to host our grown children for Christmas every year, which was important to us. It was not far from Newman, the kids' high school, and they would enjoy living in Uptown New Orleans rather than a nearby suburb. It was also close to Downtown, where I worked.

We ended up living there for about 10-12 years.

Check off finding another home in New Orleans. √ Phew!!

We did realize that we were among the "lucky" ones among the hundreds of thousands of unlucky New Orleanians, because we had the financial means to do all of the things necessary to try to rebuild our lives. The media was full of stories about the "unlucky" ones who lacked the financial means. Those were very sad, to state the obvious.

In early November, or a little over two months after Katrina, I was asked to speak to a meeting of about 75 attorneys out of town about Katrina, which I did; and during the following three to six months I was asked to speak on a few more occasions to much larger audiences of attorneys out of town about my experiences during Katrina, which I did. The title of the speech was "Katrina: Are We All Nuts?" Our emotions at the time were still raw, and the speech captured those times and our raw emotions the best. Here are some excerpts from it:

> For me, Katrina has represented another challenge and hurdle in life – a big one.
>
> The devastation of New Orleans is worse than any of you who have not seen it can imagine. It is something you have to see and experience with your own eyes and smell and senses to comprehend the scope and depth of the devastation. Many people, hundreds of thousands, have been hurt

badly, and the recovery for the city will be very slow, probably five to seven years at best and maybe ten to twenty. The Big Easy, as New Orleans is nicknamed, is not such an easy place to live any more.

* * *

Overwhelmed might best describe our response. Overwhelmed by the horrors on TV happening in our city in areas which we recognized on TV. Overwhelmed by the decisions we now had to make. Overwhelmed by being homeless! When would we be able to return to New Orleans? If ever! Where to live in New Orleans if we returned? What insurance coverages, if any, did we have for this? But those were long-term decisions on August 30th. What about work? Where should we resettle for the next months or maybe years, or maybe the rest of our lives? Should we find an apartment or buy something? In what city – Houston where we were or elsewhere where my firm had branch offices? If an apartment, what kind of lease should we sign? What about our children? Should we put them in school now for the semester which had just started? If so, where? How do we access our money without a checkbook? Online banking is something we have only since learned. Yes, we were overwhelmed that first week.

In retrospect, at the time our feelings might best be described as stunned and numb, or in a word, overwhelmed by everything. But we had each other, two of our children with us, and just did our best to take action and move forward as best we were able. Continuing with my speech:

> That fourth weekend Hurricane Rita arrived, and it became necessary to evacuate Houston for Rita. That evacuation was a painful experience. What most folks don't realize is that evacuating a city is an awful experience – sitting in heavy traffic on an interstate for 12 or 14 hours to travel what is otherwise a 3 hour trip to Austin is not fun at all, especially with children in the car and worrying about running out of gas, plus the anxiety of having to evacuate. The details are not important. But that Rita evacuation really wore on my wife and me. We had just been through hell for a month and had finally managed to get things together a little bit and then had to evacuate for Rita. But there was no damage from Rita and we were able to return to Houston the next day and enjoy one day of that fourth weekend.

It was December 17 when we returned to New Orleans. We hired movers to help us, since they would have to first load all of our things in Houston; drive it to New Orleans and unload it into the townhouse; and then load the truck again with our furniture in storage in the City and unload it too. We slept in our new home that night.

Check off returning to New Orleans. √ Phew!!

A week later we hosted our grown children for Christmas. Check off Christmas. √ Phew!!

What many people don't realize is the breadth and scope of the flooding from Katrina. It stretched from the Lake to within about one mile from the River and from the West (the Jefferson Parish line) to the East (to the St. Bernard Parish line). St. Bernard Parish, and its city of Chalmette, flooded badly too. My estimate is 200,000 to 250,000 homes flooded.

Shit happens to others in the world and in this country. It had happened to us now.

As I explained in the speech:

> Everyone in New Orleans had their own similar but unique experience. Folks evacuated all over the South. Everyone – regardless of whether their homes flooded – experienced severe hardships and have their own Katrina tales of woe. We've all learned in New Orleans to tell our Katrina story to friends in 30 seconds or less so as not to bore each other with too many details from a shared experience.

> During the first 9 weeks following Katrina, and continuing to this day (meaning early 2006) I've had to deal with some very difficult, and emotional, house issues. It turned out that our house took about 8 ½ feet of water – we lived across from the 17th Street canal and about a mile from where the levee broke. The flooding destroyed the first floor but not the second floor where we had the bedrooms and clothes. You need to

see a home that had 8 to 9 feet of water in it for three weeks to comprehend the damage and devastation. It's like a bomb went off in each room, but it's worse because of the water and the mold and the smell. We had a pink Baby Grand Piano in the living room which was upside down when we arrived. Imagine it and the other furniture floating in 8 ½ feet of water for 3 weeks. The oriental rugs were caked in mud and salt water. As my oldest daughter reminded me, the water was not just salt water from the lake but probably had chemicals and sewerage in it. It was awful.

* * *

When we went into the house, dressed in hazmat suits and gas masks and rubber boots and rubber gloves, it was worse than we expected. Seeing everything close up with your own eyes and experiencing the smell and the total devastation was unbelievable. You have to go inside a badly flooded home to comprehend it. My wife recited the prayer for the dead at the end of that day.

* * *

Losing 30 years of nice stuff and your home – your refuge – hurts a lot. It's where we raised our four children and shared so many wonderful times. Our two older children have cried more than once over the loss of the home where they grew up and still loved to visit – now just memories. Losing your home this way is like a death in a way, and you grieve your loss and feel sorry for yourself, but then you do the only thing you can, which is to move on. It still saddens us. But, and this is a big but, all of my loved ones are okay and no one I know died from Katrina.

I'm a half glass full type of guy, not a half glass empty person. I think I am A-okay mentally, emotionally, and physically. My attitude is that maybe the change will be good for me and my wife. I've never planned to retire from practicing law and I've come to realize I'm one of those who enjoy it. Nine weeks after Katrina I had landed four new major cases, some Katrina related and some not, and I have since landed lots of additional new good cases. This has energized me, and so I am doing well professionally as well as personally.

The above may help to understand how emotional and difficult this period was for most New Orleanians, no matter who you were or what you went through or how much money you had. Everyone who lived through it struggled.

There was a heated debate in New Orleans over whether or not Mardi Gras, which occurs in February usually, should go forward. The City was just starting to crawl back by then. Mardi Gras occurred. Rather than the crowds being 8-10 people deep, they were just one or two people deep. But the satire on the Mardi Gras floats, almost all about Katrina, was wonderful and uplifting and showed the spirit of the people who live in the City. It made me proud to be a native New Orleanian!

As I explained in the speech:

> Mardi Gras 2006 – the first after Katrina – reinforced for me why New Orleans is so special and unique. The humor and the satire on the Mardi Gras floats and on the costumes was emotionally uplifting. As one author wrote in the local newspaper, and I quote: "Mardi Gras has done the boldest thing imaginable: It has made art of the worst disaster in American history. Not only art – it has made comedy too. Hilarious, life-affirming, city-renewing, life-saving comedy, bursting with artistry and smarts. Is there another city on the planet whose people would respond to such a disaster with this outpouring of good humor, plus all the beads you can catch?" That's the end of the quote. It hit home for me.

Don't you just love that quote from our local newspaper? I do. It still brings tears to my eyes every time I read it. Yes, New Orleans is a very special place to live. After the trials and tribulations of Katrina, most native New Orleanians returned to live there.

Check off Mardi Gras. √ Phew!!

Jazz Fest, which occurs in late April and early May, also occurred in 2006. The crowds were sparse for it too. I remember when The Boss, Bruce Springsteen, sang My City in Ruins. It brough tears to my eyes.

I explained in the speech:

> The first Jazz Festival – with all the good music and great food and large crowds – was also very special for everyone. The local newspaper described Bruce Springsteen's singing of "My City of Ruins" as a "Jazz Fest moment for the ages" as "tears were shed." It really was.

Check off Jazz Fest.√ Phew!!

Allison did get married in April 2006, and a lot of people attended. I'm not sure how Sherrie managed to put everything together for it. Mario's (Allison's husband's) family is from Bogota, Colombia, and many of them came to it. That was a special life event for us.

Check off Allison's wedding. √ Phew!!

In September 2006, the Saints (our professional football team) played in the Superdome for the first time and won. You might remember the images on television of the "Dome" (as it is called locally) after Katrina, where many of the locals went for Katrina and the Dome's roof was badly damaged. Misery prevailed in the Dome for weeks until the people there could be relocated. When our then Lt. Governor (later our Mayor) Mitch Landrieu was asked on national television what that first game back in the Dome meant to him, he replied to this effect: "I'm a devout Catholic, and I believe in Jesus Christ, and that first game in the Dome represented the Resurrection of the City of New Orleans." I agree with his sentiment. Indeed, there was even a song by Green Day, "The Saints Are

Coming," to celebrate their return. The predominate religion of most New Orleanians was and still is Catholic.

Check off the Saints. √ Phew!!

In the Jewish religion there seems to be "rules" for almost everything. On mourning, one of the rules is to stop mourning after one year. That's easier said than done. But as time passed and it was August 29, 2006, I came to realize I was still mourning over everything we lost (our "home" of 26 years especially) and was still feeling a bit sorry for myself. I stayed home that day to watch all of the shows on television about Katrina and decided that I would stop mourning after that one-year anniversary of Katrina. It took me about another month before I stopped mourning.

That one-year maximum period to mourn in Judaism makes a lot of sense. In Judaism, it is expected that someone will mourn deeply for one week over a loss; it is also permissible to mourn deeply for one month; and it is also permissible to mourn for up to a year; but then, we are commanded to stop and to move forward. I used those rules to help me move forward.

Other Things Related to Katrina

My Dad: He was 92 at the time and didn't evacuate for Katrina. As mentioned, he never evacuated for hurricanes. A few days after Katrina we started to realize the scope of the disaster. The City was without electricity, and New Orleans was very hot at the time. His apartment had not flooded – it was located in the Sliver by the River. I called my Dad and told him the situation and that he needed to get out of town. He managed to hitch a ride to Jackson, Mississippi with a neighbor, and my daughter Allison went to the hotel where they dropped him and brought him to Shreveport to stay with my brother Carl. He continued to live in Shreveport until he died at age 99 in 2012.

While I was going to Shreveport weekly staying with Carl and Sylvia, I also got to be with my Dad every night for dinner. That was a nice thing for him and me.

The resilience of my Dad was remarkable. My Mom had been diagnosed with Alzheimer's at age 62, and he dealt with that situation until she died 17 years later (before Katrina). His lady friend after my Mom died, who he adored, also was diagnosed with Alzheimer's years later, and he had to deal with that too, which was before Katrina. Katrina no doubt was very unsettling for him, to put it mildly. The elderly were less able to deal with the disruption of Katrina. But he never complained and continued to enjoy life, or so it always seemed.

I'm sure I learned a lot from him.

<u>The Food</u>: After we returned to New Orleans and were out to dinner one night at a local, not fancy restaurant, I said to Sherrie (who was ambivalent about returning to New Orleans), "this is why we live in New Orleans," as we were enjoying a wonderful New Orleans meal, the kind that one can get in New Orleans but nowhere else in the world. Our food is that good! While the food elsewhere can be delicious too, nowhere comes close to our food.

That's my opinion, but it is shared by many locals and visitors!

As I explained in my speech:

> The good restaurants and wonderful food still remain in New Orleans. As one evacuee living elsewhere was recently quoted as saying: "There is no food like New Orleans

food. I don't care where you go in the country or around the globe. New Orleans, they just got this thing about cooking that stands alone." I agree. As he also said: "I miss so much about New Orleans. No other city can replace New Orleans. I don't say that arrogantly." I agree.

I love this quote of an evacuee from our local newspaper. It's so true.

The Soul and Uniqueness of New Orleans: New Orleans has an edginess to it that other cities lack. The mixture of our different cultures – French, Spanish, Creole, Cajun, Black, White, Italian, and Irish – creates a Gumbo (a local soup) unlike anywhere else. The street musicians play everywhere in town; the local eating places with out-of-this-world food are special; and the Mardi Gras, Jazz Fest, and other things create the soul of New Orleans. There's no place like it!

Insurance: Flooding events are excluded from homeowners' insurance policies, and the Federal flood policies only covered flooding minimally. We collected some money from our insurance policies but not nearly enough to cover our losses.

Our net financial loss was very substantial for us.

But none of our loved ones died from Katrina. We were fortunate in that regard.

The Law Practice: I learned that natural disasters are good for the law business, because a lot of people needed legal help with their insurance companies and other business matters.

While in Houston I did explore opportunities with other law firms; after all, for weeks it was uncertain if New Orleans would ever reopen at all. I had a few opportunities. But what

I came to realize quickly was that I was a Louisiana attorney in New Orleans with a good reputation nationally and locally for those in need of a New Orleans attorney. In Houston I was basically a nobody attorney without any special appeal for clients. In New Orleans I was special, and I decided that returning to New Orleans to live and work was best for me.

Katrina/Pandemic: I've often tried to compare the pandemic years (2020-2021) with Katrina to decide which was worse.

Katrina was unique to New Orleans. Everyone else felt so bad for us. I had to learn to graciously accept that sympathy from others. I was 60 at the time of Katrina, and Sherrie and I worked hard to get through it in one piece. We succeeded. Most others we know who experienced it did too.

The pandemic was a mind-fuck. The isolation and the fear of catching Covid and dying were deeply unsettling. At age 75 I resented it being imposed on us. Initially, I became angry that we had to experience and endure a pandemic in 2020 when I was 75 years old. Isn't the Number One job of our Federal government to protect us against harm, including harm against foreign enemies and against pestilence for our health? It had failed us miserably! But there was no one to blame except all politicians, Democrats and Republicans and others. My anger subsided after about a month, but I still was not a happy camper.

Learning to practice law remotely was difficult and not nearly as enjoyable as going to the office daily. Again, I was not a happy camper during it.

Both Katrina and the pandemic caused a lot of stress and anxiety.

After Katrina for weeks I found myself having a mostly sleepless night one night followed by a normal night the next, and so on. My brain was racing during the mostly sleepless nights with the problems and issues confronting us. I would address them that next day, and then slept well that night. That was anxiety, which is an excess of stress I think.

That was high stress for four months after Katrina. But I was used to high stress from work. And I handled it.

When I told my Dad that I would not have handled as well as he did if my own wife became stricken with Alzheimer's (as my Mom had at age 62), he lovingly replied yes I would have. I'm still not so sure. At least during Katrina and then the pandemic I had Sherrie around to get through them together.

I learned after Katrina how to handle some mostly sleepless nights from time to time due to anxiety, whatever the cause. Basically I accept them and try to recognize the source of the anxiety and then, as best I'm able, to deal with it. In dealing with stress and anxiety in large complicated cases, I just plow forward and do the best I can.

The anxiety from Katrina and the anxiety from the pandemic were different. During Katrina I was able to deal with the issues facing us and move forward slowly, and ultimately I was able to resolve the issues satisfactorily. During Covid I was not able to do that, because the issues were out of my control and I just had to endure it (and adjust to it) for long periods of time. But I dealt with the stresses and anxieties caused by both Katrina and Covid.

Some Final Thoughts about Katrina

I will quote other portions of my speech to try to give these final thoughts as of 2006:

> The high ground along the River which
> did not flood is now referred to by locals

as the Isle of Denial or the Sliver by the River or the Silver Sliver, because on this Isle of Denial or Sliver by the River one does not see or experience the ruins of the rest of the City. Downtown New Orleans, the French Quarter and most of the business infrastructure are part of this Sliver by the River. Many of the old institutions of New Orleans that are uptown are also located on the Sliver by the River. But other important ones flooded.

I now drive out of my house along St. Charles Avenue and am 7 minutes from my office in one direction and 5 minutes from my kids school in the other direction. As I tell my friends, out of sight out of mind, and maybe I'm out of my mind, but it is really nice to be resettled in a home with my wife and kids and to experience a routine and a sense of normalcy again. I am back to practicing law hard again. Maybe I'm living in a bubble now.

I do not enjoy driving through the ruins at all. It upsets me for days afterwards, literally, when I have to drive through the ruins and see the devastated homes with brown stains showing the flood lines – like a bathtub brown stain – and the markings on the doors from the military search and rescue mission indicating how many dead were inside and the trailers in front of homes where some folks now live among the devastation. I make an effort now to avoid driving through the ruins.

What most folks don't appreciate is the scope and depth of the devastation from the flooding. It's not a home here or a home there. It's every home in a neighborhood which was devastated from the flooding, and the devastation stretches for miles and miles – from north to south maybe 8 miles, and from east to west maybe 20 miles. About 200,000 to 250,000 homes flooded.

The greater metropolitan area of New Orleans has gone from about 1.5 million people to about 1 million. Maybe 1.2 million today. What flooded so badly was not the entire metropolitan area but, instead, about 80 percent of Orleans Parish and another smaller one, which have gone from about 550,000 people to about 175,000. Many folks have moved into neighboring parishes and now commute downtown.

* * *

For me personally, I lost my beautiful home in a beautiful neighborhood and all of the nice stuff downstairs where we lived for 26 years – a big huge bummer which still saddens me. But, other than that all is okay. I'm resettled practicing law hard again. The times are interesting and challenging in New

Orleans. Think about it: New challenges in new interesting times. Maybe, just maybe, I'm lucky in a strange way to have this new challenge in my life at age 60. Maybe I was starting to get a little stale practicing law, and maybe at age 60 I'm a little bit lucky to be facing new challenges in new interesting times.

The four months from Katrina on August 29 until the new year were the most difficult four months of my life. Everyone from New Orleans would say the same thing. It made me realize how dependent I am on my wife and family for my inner harmony and peace. It has also made me appreciate all aspects of daily living more. I've become a more sensitive person.

* * *

People from New Orleans love their city like no others I've ever met care about their city, including me. I'm not sure why – maybe it's the humor, the unique things that only happen in New Orleans, and the unique people.

The unique edgy culture and things about New Orleans – the unbelievable food and all the great neighborhood restaurants, the different music and all of the live music spots, the wonderful satire and humor, the art and architecture, the rich French and Spanish influences and history, the many fun things to do, all the funky neighborhood bars, the parades, the music festivals, the nearby fishing and hunting spots which make you feel you're in another part of the world, the beautiful oak trees uptown which are like pieces of art, the parks, the streetcars, the French Quarter, the mighty Mississippi River, all the funky people – that's why people like me still live in New Orleans and love it so much.

Today, I still feel the same about New Orleans as a great place to live. Of course, the ruins of the City from Katrina are now mostly a thing of the past. The levees have all been strengthened and improved by our Federal Government to withstand large hurricanes. Houses and other structures which were flooded have been either rebuilt or demolished, and the City is normal now. Yet, when I say normal, I mean normal for New Orleans, because New Orleans is anything but an ordinary place to live and work.

....

BOOK THREE

THE IMPORTANCE OF STRESS, ROUTINES, GAMES, FRIENDS, JUDAISM, CHRISTMAS, AND RAISING CHILDREN

My Current Stress

At age 79 (with 80 not far ahead), do I still want stress and some anxiety in my life?

The advertising portrays "retirement" as the golden age of life, worry free of anything. What a crock!

Just because I'm older doesn't mean I don't require a certain level of stress in my life. I think we all require some stress in our lives. Interacting with others is stressful in a way. Isolation can be more stressful, as we learned during the pandemic.

And along with stress comes anxiety from time to time. That anxiety is what tells us the stress level has gotten too high and needs to be adjusted. Doesn't this entire process continue until the day we die?

Enough about Katrina and the pandemic and stress/ anxiety – let's talk about more pleasant things.

Routine

Whoever came up with the idea of a five-day work week followed by a weekend for other things was brilliant in my opinion. Or, was it the weekend followed by the work week?

This construct is of course Biblical because God created the World in six days and rested on the seventh. Sometime thereafter we created calendars along with the work week and weekends.

The work week usually requires the discipline to wake up earlier, to get somewhere by an appointed time, to accomplish some form of work for the day, and then to come home. The hours of the routine vary among all the different types of work. But the basic construct is the same: The work week gives us the pleasure and ability to do or create something worthwhile, which makes us feel good about ourselves, and to be paid for our efforts. The weekend then gives us some "me time" to recharge our batteries and do whatever we want. Vacations are the same.

But, without the work week there would be no weekends or vacations. It's the ying-yang of life – you don't have one without the other.

During Katrina especially (and later during Covid too), I came to appreciate the importance of routines for my physical, mental, and emotional well-being, and I have continued to appreciate the importance of my routine for myself. Today, my routine includes eating breakfast while I read the local morning newspaper online, stretching for my back, and then shaving, showering, and dressing to go to work. I wake up early and don't rush in the morning. I do some of my best thinking during this time. When I get home from work, I change into my more comfortable clothes and relax, process the day, and get ready mentally for the next day.

Games

Games are a good distraction at times and are fun. Someone wins and someone loses. The thrill of victory and the agony of defeat, as the saying goes. It's important to learn how to win graciously and how to lose without despair. After all, isn't a big part of life about winning and losing?

When I was 22 years old, during the Summer between my having graduated college and starting law school, a friend (Peter) from a different high school and I decided we should compete in a Decathlon. A Decathlon at the Olympics involves 10 events (mostly track and field events). The winner is often considered the best athlete in the world. Rafer Johnson and Caitlyn Jenner (formerly Bruce Jenner) won it as Americans.

Peter was a basketball player, like me, and a good athlete. We devised our own private Decathlon of 10 events, which included basketball, tennis, ping pong, badminton, horseshoes, pocket pool, swimming, racing on foot, golf, and one or two others that we felt would be competitive for each of us; in most of the events we played the best of two out of three. Golf was the last event. Neither of us was good at golf.

After the first nine events our score was tied, remarkably. Neither of us wanted golf to decide who was the better athlete. So, we called our Decathlon a tie and didn't play golf.

That was fun. I have always enjoyed sports.

Golf is the only sport I've ever played that made me appreciate how non-athletes feel about sports generally. Every other sport I've ever played I was able to become good at it. Not golf, though. I did try to get better at golf when I was 12 or

13 years old, but to no avail. I just didn't have any "touch" or "feel" for the game, and found it frustrating if I scored poorly the first few holes as was usually the situation.

I recall a friend in college telling me I was the best Jewish athlete in the history of New Orleans. I had never previously considered myself to be a "Jewish" athlete. I still don't.

I also recall a good friend from high school telling me, maybe 40-50 years later, that I was his "nemesis" because I was always the better athlete and the better student. I was saddened by his sentiment. I tried to explain that I just loved to compete at everything and that it was nothing personal with him. I think I may have added, "I'm just an equal opportunity competitor." I think he understood and we remain friends.

Today (and for the last 20 years), I play the game of chess a lot. I still don't like to lose, and I can be competitive with better, more experienced chess players. I enjoy my games of chess with others.

Friends

Good friends are important, because they are the people who we like and enjoy and who we usually have fun with the most. It just takes a few. My wife is my best friend and I'm lucky in that regard. But my other best friends are important for me too, including Robert, John, Stanley, and Kathy (who has been my Secretary, now called an Administrative Asisstant, for the past 48 years). Kathy has been with me since 1976, a year after I returned to New Orleans, and has been invaluable for me. I tell her, jokingly, that she's my "work wife." My best friends keep me engaged and social, and they can be trusted, just like my brothers, and they "keep it real" for me when I say or do dumb things.

My Children

I adore my children.

My comical definition of "true love" is when you change your child's dirty diaper and get shit under your nails and don't mind it at all. There is no one else in my life I can say that about, including Sherrie. I enjoy "true love" for my children.

Our first was a girl, Tiffany. She taught me patience during her teenage years. Somehow when your children turn 13, or later, they have learned all of your buttons and press them down hard. I learned not to overreact to Tiffany when she pressed my buttons. Allison, our second child, was also challenging at times, especially when she was in her young twenties, and my parenting of her as a young adult required different, more nuanced skills than parenting Tiffany. Allison ultimately came to accept and appreciate our advices and concerns. Dustin, our only son, taught me that "true love" exists also for a male child; we have always kissed each other (on the cheek) and hugged. I always thought that was manly, especially as he aged, and he came to enjoy our man hugs. Our youngest, Brittany, insists she's our favorite, and whenever she asks me if she is my favorite, I tell her "you're my favorite at this moment, and whoever of you I'm with at the time is my favorite in that moment too." She laughs but insists she's our favorite just to be funny. As our baby we may have spoiled her the most, and she has certainly been a delight for us. I adore all four of our children the same.

There is a fine line between spoiling your children too much for their own good and welfare, on the one hand, and being too strict with them, on the other. We should want our children to be self-sufficient and independent. They want that for themselves too. When you spoil your children too much out of your love and adoration of them, you actually do them a disservice.

Our children have marveled over how well they all turned out despite their parents, Sherrie and me. The reason is the love we showered on them. They understood well how much we loved them and how everything we did for them was out of our love for them.

My Mom once told me, after I asked, that the key to raising children is to "love them to death." She was right on, I think.

The depth of our love for them still, after they have grown and married and have their own children, is enduring and sustaining in our lives. I now understand when my father used to tell me when he was in his 80's and 90's that his pride in his three boys sustained him. His pride in us was really his love for us.

Judaism

In Judaism boys and girls become adults at age 13 and usually have a Bar Mitzvah (or Bat Mitzvah for girls). The 13-year old leads the service on Saturday morning (again, our Sabbath is from sundown Friday until sundown Saturday), which includes reciting prayers in Hebrew and reading a passage from the Torah (the first five books of the Bible) in Hebrew. For the child the experience is terrifying. They spend a lot of their precious time studying to be able to perform adequately. The Synagogue is filled for the Bar or Bat Mitzvah service, which lasts about two hours. Relatives from all over the country come to town for it, and the child's friends (who are mostly not Jewish in our communities) come to the service too.

It's remarkable to me when the child performs the service so well, as is usually the case. For them, it's a huge relief.

After the service there is a luncheon at the Synagogue with mostly Jewish food. The adults get to socialize with each other. So do the children.

That evening there is a party which everyone attends. The children dance with each other, sometimes for the first time, and have a lot of fun. The adults do too.

At age 13, all this fuss is made over him or her. The child is beaming with pride and love: So many relatives coming to town just for him or her; so many friends attending too just for him or her. These warm feelings within the child certainly help to guide and sustain him or her during the difficult teenage years.

A Bar Mitzvah was not part of my childhood. Back then in the 1950's the child was required to attend Hebrew School classes after school every week day to have a Bar Mitzvah. My parents knew we loved sports, which involved practice every week day after school too, and they decided it was best for us to play sports. There were only two boys in my Newman class who had Bar Mitzvahs. Instead, I was confirmed, which is essentially a graduation service for our Sunday School class where we learned about Judaism and the Jewish holidays. My parents were raised as Orthodox Jews, which is the most religious sect of Judaism. Their "rebellion" of sorts was to switch to Reform Judaism, which is the most liberal of the religious sects of Judaism. Hence, we attended services at a Reform Synagogue, not at an Orthodox Shul (as they're called).

For the last 50 years or so, Bar and Bat Mitzvahs have been performed at Reform Synagogues for 13-year olds. We are Reform Jews. All of our children and grandchildren have performed the Bar or Bat Mitzvah service. They learned Hebrew from tutors on the weekends.

I'm strongly Jewish, but I am not religious. Sherrie is more religious. I wish in a way that I was more religious, but I just don't feel it. For me, God is the "Force" from Star Wars, which is to say I recognize there is a greater force out there but I don't know what it is. But I enjoy being Jewish and most of the Jewish traditions and food.

For me these Bar and Bat Mitzvah services of my children and grandchildren are mostly about family and friends. It's fun, enjoyable and heart-warming when we "show off" our immediate family, including our own children and our children's children, to the rest of our family and friends. Everyone is so impressed with them. The compliments we receive about them, and what a "beautiful family" we have, make us proud. There is a Yiddish term (a Jewish dialect) "kvelling," which means "bursting with pride" and is pronounced like it's spelled. Sherrie and I always kvell after these Bar and Bat Mitzvahs.

So, too, our children kvell after they see their own children perform the Bar or Bat Mitzvah service. So, too, the grandchild kvells after they perform the service admirably.

These are very special times and occasions for us.

Christmas

Sherrie and I have four children, three girls and a boy. They're very different. They love each other and us. We get together, including spouses and their children, once a year for a week over Christmas. For the past five years or so we have rented a large house in another area of New Orleans to house everyone. There are many cousins who come to New Orleans from all over the country for Christmas just to be with their New Orleans family. These times are special.

This tradition for the past 80 plus years started in a small town in Mississippi with Sherrie's grandparents, who were merchants. There is no Christmas tree and we don't celebrate Jesus Christ's birth on Christmas because we are Jewish (and different). What we do celebrate is Santa Claus! 😊

The tradition includes a row of gifts for each child younger than 13. Ori, who was 4 at the time, yelled out one Christmas morning while opening gifts, "This is AMAZING." He was right on.

I recall feeling "left out" on Christmas day growing up, because as a Jew I was not celebrating Christmas and there was very little to do that day. I might go to a movie with my parents or Jewish friends. That day drove home for me that I was different. It was not a good feeling being "left out" of the fun times that others were having that day.

After marriage to Sherrie, we have celebrated Christmas every year in a big way. Sherrie's parents and her aunts and uncles carried on the family tradition in New Orleans, which had started in a tiny Mississippi town of about 1,000 people. About seven years after we moved back to New Orleans in 1975, we continued with the tradition in our home. Sherrie's parents were devout Orthodox Jews and still loved this Christmas family tradition.

Our children insist that we continue with the tradition so that their children can have the same experiences they had. The tradition includes: All of the children under age 13 go to bed early in one room in the house that hosts Christmas after we read "The Night Before Christmas" to them; the adults then exchange gifts that evening and set up the rows of gifts for each child; early the next morning around 6:30 all of the adults are awakened and someone blows the Shofar (which is a ram's horn similar to a trumpet which Jews blow on Rosh Hashanah) to wake up the children and to let them know it's time for Christmas presents; for about an hour and a half, or longer, the children open their presents with help from their parents and others; after that, a huge "Moorhead" (the tiny Mississippi town where the tradition started) breakfast is served, which includes eggs, bacon (yes bacon), sausages, biscuits, and molasses, and is always a special meal; and then everyone just hangs out playing with the gifts and being together.

It's a special morning, and then in the afternoon we all get together in a relative's home for a seafood lunch and football on the levee at the Lake.

So, I went from feeling left out on Christmas day until I was 26 (when I married Sherrie) to enjoying the most wonderful day of celebration that one can imagine with my family. And, we celebrate Santa Claus and being with family!

I'm sure this special day is part of the glue of my marriage and of my family too.

Raising Children

My father-in-law told me once that the more time and effort I spent raising my children, the more of a reward I would enjoy from doing so. My wife Sherrie really spent the most time raising our children. I was a hard-working attorney during those years. But, in the early mornings and evenings I would always spend time with them helping them get ready for school, driving them to school for years, having family dinner with them and asking them to tell me about their day, and just relaxing watching TV with them. They were good company for me.

I also tried to attend their sporting or other extra-curricular activities when I could.

I disliked traveling for work and missing whatever was going on in their lives, but duty called and I traveled when necessary.

I had no idea of everything involved with raising children, including the expenses, but Sherrie guided me along as if she knew what was best. She was usually right, but not always. That would cause friction between us, and we would argue in front of our children at times. They learned young that this was just our way and we were not getting divorced. They didn't like when we argued in front of them and they still don't, but we still do it. They've come to know us well.

When the children became teenagers, Sherrie was "all over them" and wanted to be sure to protect them. I was less concerned given all of my crazy stunts at that age, not that Sherrie didn't have them too. We became sort of the good cop/bad cop with them. But when I became upset with them and put my foot down so to speak, they understood and backed down usually. Not always though, especially as they got older.

Remember the Excedrin commercial, "I have a headache this big and it has Excedrin written all over it"? My oldest, Tiffany, used to love that commercial and repeat it to me. One day, though, she told me, "Dad, I have a headache this big and it has Mom written all over it." I laughed, but she was asking for help with Sherrie. I went to the room where Sherrie was and said, what is going on between Tiffany and you? She asked why I asked? When I told her what Tiffany said to me, Sherrie laughed hard like I did. She went into the room where Tiffany was and hugged her.

The American Dream?

Think about this: I'm a Jew living in a land called America; I'm also an American citizen who enjoys all the same rights and privileges of other Americans; I've had lots of success in my chosen profession and with my family; I'm still doing what I enjoy and want to do every week day; and I still have my wife Sherrie who loves me dearly, and I adore her too.

It wasn't easy at all getting to this point. I worked hard along the journey. I came to value hard work because it seemed to reward me more often than not.

So, let's revisit some of this journey of Alan.

....

BOOK FOUR

JOURNEY OF ALAN

The Early Years: Up to Age 14

I would say that for my first 14 years I was just a regular child. I was fortunate, though, to be the youngest of my parents' children, because my brothers led the way for me with my parents and looked out for me along the way, and my parents had more money as they and we aged. Thus, I enjoyed certain advantages that my brothers did not, such as starting at Newman school when I was in third grade while they did not start there until seventh grade (for Carl) and sixth grade (for Malcolm). There were other fringe benefits I enjoyed as a result also.

Until I was 12 my parents (who were then 43 and 42) always rented where we lived, but we never wanted of anything important growing up.

I have no bad memories from this period. I did not learn about the Holocaust until I was older, maybe 13 or 14. I recall my parents talking about Israel in the 1950's when I was a child. They were very concerned for Israel, but it was not until I was older that I learned about the Holocaust.

In high school one summer I read the book, "The Rise and Fall of the Third Reich," which is over 1,200 pages. It is chilling to read. Years later I continued to read books and watch movies about the Holocaust. About 20 years ago, though, I decided I would not watch any more movies about it. They were just too upsetting for me.

When I was younger than 10, maybe 5 or 6, my older brother Carl and his friends taught me a bunch of cuss words, although I had no idea of their meaning, and I started going around in pre-school using them freely, saying "fuck," "shit," "son of a bitch," and others. This continued for a while, and my brother and his friends thought it was funny. When my parents found out what I was doing, they didn't know what to do and apparently talked with our Rabbi, as if he would know. On his advice, my father, Carl, Malcolm and I met in Carl's bedroom, and my Dad in a solemn way tried to explain their meaning to me (which I didn't understand at all), and to explain that they were bad words which I shouldn't use. I did understand they didn't want me using those words any longer, and I stopped.

When I was 12 or 13, I recall one Friday being punished, probably for talking back to one of my parents about something, and being sent to my room and not being allowed to go to a movie that night. I was planning to meet a girl there and was upset. Steaming over the punishment, I left my room very quietly and snuck out the back door to walk to the movie theater. About an hour later my Dad went there, saw me and waved for me to come with him, and we walked home. They could hardly believe I had actually done that, and were actually worried about me, and for years they would tell their friends the story in front of me, as if it was funny to them. But it wasn't funny at all to me. I don't recall any further punishment from that episode except for my total humiliation over being caught.

I guess I was bold and brash even as a child.

Indeed, when my brother Malcolm and I were campers one summer we got into a fight over a pocket pool or ping pong game, and I threw a cueball at him. When the counsellors broke up the fight and learned we were brothers, they told us both to "cool down" and made us shake hands. I guess I was also extremely intense and competitive even before Coach Tuohy entered my life. I would also compete in ping pong with my brother Carl's friends, who were 8 years older than I was, and I could play competitively with them and even won sometimes. Yes, I had a fun childhood.

I have a math mind. In first or second grade the school that I was attending wanted me to skip a grade "because I was so smart." My parents said no to the school. As my Mom later explained, the reasons for the decision were they wanted me to stay with my age group and didn't want me to be a year younger than my classmates. That seemed to be the correct decision.

My Mom never went to college. Back then, girls were not encouraged to do so. Times sure have changed for the better. My Mom was a wonderful mother, I always thought: She was very loving, liked to cook and take care of us, and had a lot of common sense. My Dad was lucky to have her, just as I'm lucky to have Sherrie.

My brothers and I were all good students. I'm not sure why. We were also all good athletes.

I recall playing biddy basketball (where the ball is smaller and the goal is lower) and then regular basketball, and I was the only one who could dribble the ball well and shoot well. If our team scored 25 points, I probably had 20 of them. I also recall going to a game of the Harlem Globetrotters, who were worldwide icons known for their basketball skills and their family entertainment, and watching Reece "Goose" Tatum (the center and a comic) and Marques Haynes (a fantastic dribbler of the ball). The next day I went to the gym and tried to dribble the ball like Haynes did. In short, even at a young age I was inspired to learn to dribble well and to shoot well.

I am a classic overachiever, meaning that based on my abilities and short stature I somehow managed to achieve more success than my abilities warranted. That may just be the natural result of my being the youngest and watching my brothers in their sports and observing my parents urging them to study harder in school.

The Magical Years: Ages 15-17

I had two magical years, one at age 15 and then again at age 17. I really did, no shit.

During the summer when I turned 15, before my Sophomore year of school, I was playing a lot of tennis after my summer job, and decided I would start playing in tennis tournaments to compete. Some of them were out of town but still in Louisiana, and I would travel to them with other New Orleans tennis players who were older. I came to realize that I was not that good of a tennis player and did not enjoy the tournaments so much. Truth be told, I was a better athlete than most of the other players, but my tennis skills were not as strong as the others, and when I won a match it was due to my just being a better athlete.

For example, I won the City Championship Tournament for kids 15 and younger, even though there were several players who were more skilled in tennis. That was fun for me, of course, but there was an aspect of tennis I did not enjoy so much, and that was it was just me alone competing against others because tennis is not a "team sport" in the traditional meaning of team sports. That may also have been because I never had a tennis coach to teach me to be better. I enjoyed football, basketball, and baseball team sports more than tennis (and I had coaches for them). Being short of stature, I probably could have been more successful if I had stuck with tennis as my main sport, but I just didn't enjoy it as much.

It was that summer when the newly hired varsity coach of Newman, Coach Tuohy, called me and invited me to practice with the Newman varsity team in football. Back then, Sophomore students rarely played on the varsity teams with the Juniors and Seniors. Varsity football practice always started August 15 each summer, and practices were twice a day for 2-3 weeks in the early mornings and late afternoons due to the extreme heat and humidity in the City.

We didn't even have 22 players for practice and the games. When we scrimmaged at practice, we would first work on the right side of the line on offense and defense and then on the left side. Imagine that, having to practice offense and defense first for the right side and then the left side.

Coach Tuohy decided that I should compete for three positions – namely, quarterback, defensive safety, and punter. My competition included the Juniors and Seniors, and I ended up winning the starting quarterback, the starting safety, and the punter positions. I also returned kickoffs and punts. I was loving playing varsity football and hanging out with the older players. In games we played both offense and defense without ever going out of games, even when we were exhausted, with the only exception being if we were hurt.

Coach Tuohy had previously coached at Holy Cross High School, a much larger school than Newman that was in a rough neighborhood of the City and a powerhouse in football. He arranged for us to scrimmage Holy Cross one afternoon at its field. We were scared shitless to face them. Coach told us they "put their pants on one leg at a time, just like we did," and we had nothing to fear. That didn't really help. But during that scrimmage we competed fiercely, and held our own so to say, although they did better clearly. What we learned that day was that we could compete with the best New Orleans had to offer.

In the first game of the season in September, I was knocked out, rendered unconscious briefly, and couldn't remember where I was or what happened. I probably had a concussion from the hit to my head (yes, we wore helmets). After sitting out for a few series I started to regain my bearings, and Coach sent me back into the game.

We won the game.

Our second game was against a much better team from another city. We played the game there. I recall when Coach called our Quarterback Flare play, which is when I would pitch the ball to a halfback (a running back) and go out for a pass the other way. The halfback overthrew the ball to me, and I ran as fast as I could and dove to catch the ball in the end zone before sliding out of bounds. Touchdown!!

We won that game too.

None of our games were easy for us. I remember one game when we were up 12-7 but were deep into our own end of the field and had to punt out of the end zone. The other team was running the ball well and it seemed we were going to lose the game. I called a timeout and suggested to Coach that we purposely take a safety, which would still make the score 12-9 in our favor, but which would allow us to punt the ball to the other team from our 20-yard line instead of from deep in our own end zone, or a 30-yard difference. Coach liked the idea. Our defense stiffened after that punt of 40 or so yards from our 20-yard line, and we won the game.

After winning our first 4-5 games we played the best team at the time, Buras, which was south of New Orleans in a small town along the bayous of Louisiana. Their students were basically shrimpers and Cajuns who were tough and good. We were losing 12-7, time was running low, and we were marching close to their end zone. It was fourth down. Coach called a running play for one of our co-captains of the team. I changed the play in the huddle, which Coach said I could do any time. The co-captain protested, but I told him to shut up, and we made the first down from the play I called. We scored soon afterward and won the game 13-12.

That was gutsy and brash of me, a mere Sophomore among Seniors. Coach taught us to be brash. I simply followed his lead.

That year we went undefeated, 8-0, in football, something Newman had never done previously and still hasn't. But unlike the later Newman teams when Peyton and Eli Manning and Odell Beckham, Jr. played, we did not compete for the State Championship.

After football season ended, we started practice for basketball. Again, Sophomores rarely played varsity sports back then, and Coach invited me to play varsity basketball too. The team was mostly Seniors, a few Juniors, and me.

I ended up as a starting guard in basketball, beating out two Seniors for the position, and our five starters were four other Seniors and me. That of course was fun for me.

In New Orleans there was a Catholic League at the time consisting of much larger schools than Newman with bigger and better players too. That first year Coach scheduled us to play all of the Catholic Schools -- except for one which refused because, we were told, they didn't want to risk losing to a smaller, academically stronger school -- before our league (called Riverside) started playing against each other. We beat all of them. After we beat the best Catholic League team, Coach came into the locker room and told us, "Well, you uptown fruits did it again!!" He was beaming with pride. Coach Tuohy was an Irish Catholic from the poorer part of Chicago, and he was a coach for one of the Catholic Schools before he came to Newman. After we won against the best school in the Catholic League, the local newspaper (The Times Picayune) ran a headline "Newman Crowned Catholic Champs." The irony of that headline was that many of our players were Jewish, which was never mentioned publicly.

I recall another basketball game that year against another Catholic League team. I was not having a good game and had picked up 4 fouls. One more foul and I would be out of the game. We were behind 13 points after 3 quarters of play. I scored 12 points the last quarter, including our last 4 of the game, and we won by a point.

Yes, I was brash too, like Coach Tuohy.

That year in basketball we went undefeated, 32-0, and won the State Title.

It was March of 1961 when the basketball season ended. Football and basketball were the only two varsity sports in which Newman competed. Our teams went 40-0 that year.

I remember the school assembly after we won every game. The Headmaster introduced Coach Tuohy, and Coach then addressed the entire school. He was masterful and everyone loved him. He was a winner for sure, and Newman had never previously enjoyed so much success in sports and so much school spirit from winning that much. It was exhilarating!!

As for me, I was still a 15-year old kid trying to find and make my way along with everyone else. I also knew that it was important for me to continue to study hard and make good grades in school. My parents and older brothers kept me grounded.

I did not ever feel I was better than others in my class or school. I was just having fun, doing my thing, along with my classmates.

In retrospect, I now realize that my Sophomore year

at Newman was magical and one for the ages. At the time, though, I was just enjoying the year.

My Junior year, our Newman teams were not as good. In football we were just average. In basketball, though, thanks to a rising star one year younger than I was, we managed to go 29-7 and got to the semi-finals of the State tournament before losing.

Academically, though, I did extremely well my Junior year, ending the year with all A+'s and A's in my courses of study.

I recall a math class where the teacher taught us Sines, Co-Sines, and Tangents, which are important in Trigonometry. She explained Sines and put the formula on the chalkboard. She then asked the class to try to figure out the formula for Co-Sines. I did and explained the formula to the class as she wrote it on the chalkboard. To this day, I have no idea how the logic for Co-Sines came to me, but it did. When the teacher then asked the class to try to figure out the formula for Tangents, giving us a clue, I explained that formula to the class too. The teacher was impressed and asked me if someone had explained the formulas to me. I replied no, which is the truth. I still don't know why math came so easily for me, but it did. I never studied for math tests or exams, except maybe to review quickly what we had been taught, and I usually got 100 on them.

I was proud of my academic achievements my Junior year. Those grades would help me to get into the best colleges in the Country. Newman had a strong reputation for academics and was familiar to the top colleges.

My Senior year was magical again. I had decided after my Junior year that I wanted to get better at basketball and practiced hard all summer. I did not like losing in the semi-finals of the State Tournament my Junior year. Coach Tuohy helped by asking one of his colleagues at one of the Catholic schools to coach me. I think my parents paid him to coach me.

I took public transportation (city buses) every afternoon to and from the tutor's school's gym, which took about 45 minutes each way, and spent about two hours each day learning to shoot better. Each evening after dinner, I would go back to the gym to play pick-up basketball with other older kids who were more proven players. I worked hard to improve my game and did. I was competing with other better players and held my own most of the time.

In football I got hurt in the second game of my Senior year (shoulder separation) and was out for the season. I was crushed emotionally because I had ambitions to play both football and basketball in college, something that was rarely done back then and today. I had gotten much better in football too that summer, and had learned to become a roll-out quarterback which allowed me to pass better (due to my short stature) even on the run and the option to run around the end too. I was playing well in practice and in our first game. But that injury in the second game ended my football season and aspirations.

Basketball it would be for my Senior year. Our team was very good again, thanks mostly to some Juniors who were very good, including one taller guy Bobby (6 feet, 3 inches) who could shoot well and was our best player. He and I led that team to another undefeated season, 32-0 again coincidentally, and we won State again.

On that team our center on offense, Bob, was only 5 feet 7 ½ inches tall. He was excellent on defense as a guard, and was scrappy and quick and could jump, but he was not very good at dribbling or shooting the ball beyond 10 feet. Coach came up to me before practice early in the season and said, "Alan, I'm thinking of playing Bob at center. Tell me if I'm crazy."

I replied: "I've been thinking the same thing. We could play Bob (my height) at center on offense so that Bobby (our 6 feet 3 inches tall guy who could shoot well) could play forward and score more points; and then Bob and I would play guards on defense and wreak havoc and disrupt the other teams and Bobby (taller) could play center on defense if the other teams got past Bob and me." It worked remarkably well, and our success that year was due more to our tenacious man-to-man defense than to our offense. But even on offense, we were able to score well because our short center Bob learned to shoot well closer to the goal when teams double-teamed Bobby or me and we passed the ball to Bob. That was a very good team and was undefeated and State champions, just like the team two years earlier.

In my three years of basketball at Newman, we went 93-7 and never lost a home game in our gym. The banner we had posted my Sophomore year in the gym reading "Welcome to Death Valley" remained there and rang true.

In my academics I continued to do well too. I was accepted to the Honors Math class my Senior year where we learned Calculus. At our year-end graduation, I received the Math Award for our class.

I was also the Second Honor Student of our class at graduation.

I was probably prouder of being the Second Honor Student than being All-State in basketball. Newman was considered the best school academically in the City, and had a good reputation nationally with the top colleges, and applicants had to pass a rigorous exam just to be accepted. My academic side has endured and blossomed through the years. Athletically, I'm a mere shell of my former self, though, due to my being age 79 and counting. My exercise now is to walk 1 ½ miles three days a week and light weights once a week.

My Senior year of high school was thus magical, too, similar to my Sophomore year.

Indeed, when I see former classmates and friends from around the City, those high school years often become a topic of conversation. Sometimes when I meet someone for the first time and tell them my name, they ask if I'm the same person who played for Newman. Those conversations are always fun for me.

It's also worth mentioning some of the new controversial and brash customs Coach Tuohy started at Newman during his first year when I was a mere Sophomore to motivate us.

First, he required that his players run (not walk) off the field or court after each game (win or lose) without shaking hands with the other team. Some of the parents (including mine) questioned this new rule of Coach, but we kept winning and they stayed quiet. As Coach told us, the other team was our enemy and he didn't want us to be friendly with them. Okay, that made sense – our goal was to beat the enemy and we did.

Second, he required on game days in basketball that his players wear a green sportscoat (Newman's colors were green and white) with the school's name "Isidore Newman School" emblazoned on it, plus a tie. All of his players thus stood out on game days in classy style.

Third, in basketball during warmups we used green and white basketballs (two of them) for the lay-ups to get ready to play. Not only that, he had us run out of the locker room – but only after the other team had started its warmups – in a big circle at the start of our lay-ups. No doubt, the other team saw us acting brashly but in a stylish way. Remember, we also posted the large banner in our gym saying "Welcome to Death Valley."

Coach Tuohy may have been rough around the edges (some might say), but he certainly brought style and class to his teams, and we won our games mostly during my three years of high school. As we continued to win during his first year, more and more students and others attended the games, to the point where our own gym would be packed full with spectators with standing room only for many. Newman had never previously enjoyed so much school spirit and support for its sports teams.

Coach Tuohy started a new wave of school spirit that the school still enjoys. I was there with him those first few years.

I should mention that my intensity in sports (and in other things) helped me a lot but sometimes got me in trouble. I hated to lose, like Coach Tuohy, and would get angry (never at my teammates) when we weren't doing well during a game, and that intensity drove me harder and harder to do everything possible to find a way to win the game, which we usually did. Once or twice I got into fights with the opposing team's players when they taunted me, and I recall even being ejected in one game. The local newspaper sometimes called me "angry Al Goodman." I didn't like being called that, or being taunted by opposing players, but I never backed off, because winning was that important for me. My parents told me that I should try to control my anger better, and I did, but I remained just as intense inwardly while trying not to show my anger outwardly. I'm sure I still showed my extreme intensity during those times.

I will reiterate that my extreme intensity usually led to my finding a way to win, both in sports and in life. I was determined and had the drive to win, almost as if it was a matter of life or death, and usually did find a way to win. It was not so much that I loved to win. It was that I hated, and I mean HATED, to lose.

In fact, I hated losing so much that if we did lose I was glad to run off the court (or field) without shaking hands with the other team's players, as Coach directed us to do.

Even today, I hate to lose in my legal cases and can usually find a way to win or, if our case is not strong, to extract a decent settlement for the client. I'm sure others saw this intensity of mine which combined with my smarts almost always led to good results.

I recall one of Newman's much younger, star basketball players telling me years later that Coach Tuohy had told him that he "needed to be more like Alan Goodman," and that he needed more fire in his belly. I did have "fire in my belly" for sure, and that no doubt helped us to win.

It's also worth mentioning that I enjoyed dating girls a lot during these three years. At age 15 in New Orleans, I was able to get a driver's license (the age is now 16), and that gave me the freedom to date and to "make out" (mostly "kissy face" back then) with my dates privately in the family car if there was mutual attraction. That was a lot of fun for me – driving a family car at night to pick up my date, talking and doing fun things with my date like going to a movie or sports event, and then "making out" if there was mutual attraction before taking the date home. I had different girlfriends during these years, some more serious than others, and was just having fun and enjoying myself. I didn't drink alcohol until after the basketball season my senior year ended, and that added to the fun too.

We did some wild things during those years, but it was all to have fun. We were not juvenile delinquents, but today some of our stunts would no doubt be frowned upon. We of course never mentioned any of this to our parents, and it was fun being "bad."

In other words, I was a normal teenager and was enjoying myself a lot, even while I worked so hard in my sports and academic endeavors.

Yes, these were magical years!!

Alan

The Come Down Years: Ages 18–22

At Newman the best students in each class were encouraged to attend colleges like Harvard, Yale, M.I.T., Columbia and the like. In my Senior class, students attended all of these and others. Even average students attended other excellent colleges out of town like Brown, Dartmouth, Washington University (in St. Louis), Vanderbilt, Emory, Virginia, Wesleyan, and others. Our school principal was upset that I wasn't considering any of them. The reason, of course, was that I had been offered a full athletic scholarship to Tulane to play basketball and accepted it.

The scholarship was a really big deal for my parents. They didn't have the money of the other parents of my Newman classmates, and sending me away for college would have been a big expense for them. Plus, my Dad and his brother attended Tulane, as did my brothers Carl and Malcolm. "Why isn't Tulane good enough for you?" my Dad asked.

I was excited over the opportunity to play major college basketball in the SEC in my hometown of New Orleans at Tulane. My parents agreed I could live in a dormitory and eat my meals with the other athletes (football, basketball, baseball, and tennis players), which was all part of the scholarship and would be free too, and which would be sort of like living out of town for college. My parents also bought me a cheap used car after my freshman year, which enabled me to have more fun too.

At Newman I didn't go to the French Quarter much, which is the area of New Orleans well known for its strip clubs and live music spots and drinking booze on the streets. At Tulane the other players and I would go to the French Quarter and to the bars and live music spots often. Our favorite was Pat O'Brien's, a famous bar off of Bourbon Street, where the entertainer (Emile) would introduce us to the crowd because he admired Tulane athletes so much. While the French Quarter was considered seedy and unsafe in areas, I always felt safe walking around with the other much taller and bigger players and going to bars where fights would break out on rare occasions among drunken sailors or soldiers or locals. All the bars had "bouncers" to eject rowdy patrons.

I also joined a fraternity at Tulane, ZBT, which is the one my brothers had joined. While I never lived at the fraternity house, I did enjoy ZBT and its members a lot, including going to its parties on the weekends and eating lunch there occasionally.

I also still dated girls a lot on the weekends.

My Mom was nevertheless concerned (correctly in retrospect) that I had enjoyed so much success at Newman that any college experience would be a let down (or come down) for me. Even if I had attended Harvard or Yale, the same come down would surely have occurred. That I was in New Orleans for the come down, in my familiar City, was probably a good thing and made my come down a bit softer than might have been the case elsewhere out of town.

While I felt important at Tulane being on a basketball scholarship and playing in the same Tulane gym where as a kid I watched Tulane basketball games, I learned quickly that I was just one of thousands of students at Tulane and was not as special as I had been at Newman. It was at Tulane where I learned to compete in a broader world with others; Newman was a small school compared to Tulane; and I learned I still could compete at Tulane and started to mature as an adult.

In basketball, I was not a star. I was just too short, and there was not a 3-point shot back then which would have made a huge (and I mean HUGE) difference for me. That was disappointing. In short, playing college basketball, and being mostly a backup rather than a starting guard, was a come down for me. I could make excuses: My Freshman year we were not allowed to play varsity, and I did start on our Freshman team. My Sophomore year I became ill with Mononucleosis at the beginning of the season which set me back a lot. My Junior year I did work up to starting on the team and was playing well until I got in trouble with our coach later in the season, when he falsely accused me of organizing an outing after an away game -- a story not worth telling in more detail, except that I was extremely pissed off after that season when I first learned of his false accusation -- where all of us broke a curfew, and he unfairly demoted me to being a backup guard due to his false accusation (which, again, I didn't learn until the season ended) unlike the others who still started at their positions. My Senior year I broke my nose badly at practice and was out the first half of that season. I was bitter at the coach over his false accusation, but there was nothing I could do about it other than quit the team and lose my scholarship, which I didn't want to do. I did consider him a "piece of shit" due to his false accusation and for not confronting me about it at the time. When the season ended and I raised the issue with him, he only told me then but it was too late to undo it.

But these excuses aside, I was probably not good enough (and was too short) to be a star in a major college basketball program in the SEC without there being a 3-point shot, as there has now been for decades.

In my academics, I did manage to graduate *Cum Laude* (an academic honor) but, again, my grades fell off, I felt. One reason was due to basketball, because on road trips to play other teams (every other week basically) I had to miss classes on Mondays, Tuesdays, and Fridays. I did bring my class books with me, and studied on the trips when I could, but the distractions were many.

There were other distractions in New Orleans too, including my joining the fraternity and enjoying that social life too much perhaps. But this was college, and I wanted to enjoy my Tulane college years like everyone else, which I had been told was important, and I did.

After I graduated from Tulane, and as I prepared for my next stage of life, which was law school, I also came to realize this about myself: To be happiest, I would need to achieve at a higher level than I had at Tulane.

It is worth mentioning that one advantage of my attending Tulane was that I was free during the summers to experience other parts of America and the World for months at a time. Prior to my Freshman year, I drove with two high school friends (Bob, our center my Senior year, and Jack) for about five weeks to California to experience Los Angeles and San Francisco, and then to Sun Valley, Idaho to spend time there before driving home. That was fun.

Prior to my Sophomore year, I spent two months being a camp counsellor (for pay) in upper Wisconsin and enjoyed that experience a lot. I recall seeing the amazing Northern Lights flash across the sky late one night. In the camp competition between two evenly divided teams of all the older campers I acted as the coach for one of the teams; after our team won, I was "traded" to the other team to coach it in an effort to make the teams more equal; and that team then won too with me as its coach. That summer was a lot of fun.

Prior to my Junior year, I spent most of the summer in New York City with my friend Robert working as a "soda jerk" at Schrafft's, a well-known establishment. We sublet an apartment close to Columbia University on 110th Street. I met a girl from Scotland while there who I enjoyed dating, and I also enjoyed living in New York City and learning my way around it. Later that summer I went to Cape Cod in Massachusetts and experienced it too; I met another girl there who I enjoyed dating too. I recall working two different jobs while there (one being a dishwasher in a small joint). After a couple of weeks we traveled together north to Quebec, Canada, and then to Niagara Falls, and then to her home in Michigan, after which I drove home. That summer was fun too.

Prior to my Senior year, I taught basketball in Europe with my friend Bob and then traveled around Europe with him with the money I earned for about six weeks. I met a girl on the French Riviera who spoke no English, and my French speaking skills improved. That was fun too.

Those were all wonderful summer experiences for me.

While my come down at Tulane was not enjoyable, and was disappointing, and was even painful in ways, I did enjoy the summer experiences a lot.

It is also worth mentioning that I fell in love with a Catholic girl (Susan) during my Junior year. That created a major problem for her and me, even though we adored each other. Her religion was important to her, and being Jewish was important for me. Neither of us was able to envision giving up our religion and still being happy, or even sharing each other's religion and still being happy. I recall dropping her off at church one day, and she asked me to go with her. I declined, because I knew I would not be comfortable sitting in church with her while she prayed to Jesus Christ who is not part of Judaism. Her parents were vehemently against her dating a Jew, and she told me that. I also knew my parents would not approve if I married her, although I never discussed the subject with them. Despite these problems for us – religious and family – we continued to date and enjoyed our times together.

It was the next year when we broke up, because her parents insisted that she transfer to an out-of-state university to get away from me. While we continued to talk by phone and to see each other when she came home, that long distance relationship was not working for either of us. That was painful for me, and her too, but we both came to realize that our families and our religions were so important to us that we would never be happy long term if we got married.

Truthfully, it was only after I attended law school in Washington, D.C. that we had both truly moved on. I recall seeing her over Christmas during my first year of law school, and having a lot of fun with her being together, but after that we never saw each other again. It was for the best, as we both knew.

It was time to move on with my life.

The Law School and Vietnam War Years – Lots of Drama: Ages 22–25

I did explore other career paths for myself during my Senior year at Tulane. One alternative was to try to get into a military reserve unit (Army, Navy, and Air Force had them) for six months to avoid being drafted during law school. The Vietnam War was raging at the time, and college graduates no longer were able to avoid the military draft for the first time by attending graduate school. I applied to several reserve units.

I also seriously considered the option after Tulane of pursuing graduate school in my major, Political Science. I would get a Master's Degree or Ph.D. in it. The life of a college professor seemed appealing to me, except for the low pay.

I also decided my Senior year that if I went to law school, as my Dad encouraged me to do, I wanted to go out of town for it at a higher ranked school than Tulane (even though I was offered an academic scholarship to attend it). Because my academics had slid a bit at Tulane, I was not a candidate for Harvard or Yale or the other highest ranked law schools. But I applied to Georgetown in Washington, D.C., which was highly ranked (top ten), and I was accepted.

I finally decided law school would be best for me. My Dad thought it would be a good fit for me, because I had both the strong academics to do well in law school and the competitive drive to work hard and succeed at it. He was correct. As I would learn later, practicing law involves learning too, which I always enjoyed. When you're presented with a new matter (a case), the first step is to learn and understand the facts and then to learn and apply the law to them. Clients seek advice from attorneys when they can't figure things out for themselves, or when they are in litigation with others. Litigation is the ultimate dispute-resolution process in America, rather than other violent means. Litigation is considered the "civilized" way to resolve disputes, and litigation and practicing law can be very stressful at times, just like life itself.

In mid-August of 1967, which was shortly before I would be leaving to attend Georgetown, I was accepted in a Reserve Unit (Air Force). I called my Dad to seek his advice. He suggested I go ahead with my plans to attend Georgetown and said "everything would turn out okay" for me. I followed his advice (perhaps foolishly in retrospect) and came within a hair of being drafted by the Army out of law school during my first year at Georgetown.

My first year of law school was daunting. I had nowhere

to live and no good friends who attended it. After looking a bit, I rented the third floor of a home in the Georgetown area of D.C. I had heard that it was an old, neat area in D.C., somewhat similar to our French Quarter. The law school was downtown in D.C. and not on the Georgetown University campus, but I could drive there in my used car.

I was excited to be in D.C. After all, I was a Political Science major at Tulane and was interested in government. I was also excited to be at Georgetown Law Center (as it was called) among some of the brightest minds in the country. I was also excited to be away to live on my own for the first time ever (except summers when I experienced other parts of the Country and World).

In 1967 at Georgetown Law, I decided that I wanted to excel in school and make the Law Journal (same as Law Review at other law schools) which is offered only to students in the top 5-10 percent of the class. I studied my ass off and didn't have the distractions of playing college basketball, which was very time-consuming, and of fraternity life, which was very social. My only job, so to speak, was to do well at Georgetown my first year and to make the Law Journal.

After classes began, I learned for the first time (a) that we did not have exams at the end of the first semester (with one very minor exception), (b) that we didn't even have tests to take during the year, (c) that class participation counted for zero towards our grades, and (d) that our grades would be strictly based on how well we did on 4-hour exams in each course at the end of the school year in May 1968. Those were the rules of the game at hand. If there was one thing I had learned to do well, it was to play and win at games. I was driven to achieve at a high level because I knew I would be happier if I succeeded. I was also driven by the fact that my entire future in law would be determined in large part by how well I did that first year.

The Vietnam War was still raging. In February or March of 1968 I received a notice from the United States Government to attend a physical for the Army, which meant that I would be drafted into the Army if I passed the physical. I had already signed up for the D.C. National Guard but there was a long waiting list for it. If accepted, I figured I would prefer the D.C. National Guard to going to Vietnam to fight and possibly be killed or maimed.

There was a race of sorts to see who would take me first, the U.S. Army or the D.C. National Guard. Either way, I would need to suspend my law studies for at least a year. I had also considered claiming "conscientious objector" status because I was opposed to the War in Vietnam, or moving to Canada to avoid the draft, but rejected those alternatives for me. While I was strenuously opposed to our Country's involvement in what seemed to be a civil war in the Far East between the North and South of Vietnam, I was not so thoroughly convinced I was right that I felt I could honestly object in good conscience to serving in the Army as a "conscientious objector." Others viewed "conscientious objectors" as traitors of America. I certainly did not want to be labeled as a traitor of our Country. I also did not want to move to Canada and be subject to arrest as a "draft dodger" if I ever visited New Orleans. Neither choice was attractive to me. Plus, I was smart and a good athlete, and my rationale at the time was that if I did have to go to Vietnam for the War I would somehow manage the situation and avoid getting myself maimed or killed.

All of this turmoil for me personally was happening while I was studying hard for my final exams in May. It was unsettling of course, but I remained focused on my studies.

After I received the Army notice for a physical, I called my Dad and asked him to obtain a letter from our doctor in New Orleans explaining (a) that I had had major surgery on my left knee after high school, which was true (and without any mention that I played four years of college basketball on the knee), (b) that my right knee was bad too, which was true too (it had started to hurt while playing basketball), and (c) that my left shoulder had suffered a bad separation from high school football, which was also true. At the Army physical I gave the letter to them. A few weeks later the Army called and asked me to attend a second physical to meet with an Orthopedist, a specialist in knees and shoulders.

At that visit with the Orthopedist he said to me, "I see you're from New Orleans," and what a great city it was and how he had great memories from visiting it. That was encouraging. I replied, "yes sir." He then commented that I had two bad knees and one bad shoulder, and asked if that was correct. I replied again, "yes sir." He finally said, "Son, do you want to go in the Army?" I replied, "no sir." That was the end of that doctor visit, and he said I would be hearing from the Army within a couple of weeks. I had no idea what I would be hearing, though.

Shortly after that visit, the D.C. National Guard called me to say I had moved up on the waiting list and to ask if I was still interested in it. I replied, "yes sir."

The race was on. A couple of weeks later I received a notice from the Army that I was "1-Y," which meant I was physically disqualified to be admitted to the Army.

Halle-fucking-lujah!!

A week or so later the D.C. National Guard called me to say I had been accepted and to report for duty. I respectfully replied, "no thank you."

That was a lot of drama for me as I was studying hard for

my final exams. But was I relieved!! How was that for some luck?? In retrospect, I should have accepted the offer to enlist in the Air Force Reserve Unit back in the summer before law school started, but I didn't. And as a result, I never had to take a year off from my studies to deal with the Vietnam War, as many of my Tulane classmates had done to avoid military service. In retrospect again, I did create my own "luck" by having the presence of mind to obtain the letter from my Orthopedist in New Orleans and to provide it at the Army physical. My Dad turned out to be correct; this would work out okay for me. It did!!

After my final exams that first year at Georgetown Law, for which I had studied hard, I was convinced that I had not done well in them and was concerned I may have even failed one of them. My attitude, though, was that I gave it my best "college try" and what will be is what will be.

I found a summer job in D.C. working in a warehouse. I wanted to sweat my way through the summer, literally, and expunge my body of all the stress I had endured. I met a girl from Finland who I dated and liked a lot. I had been told it would probably be July before I knew my law school grades.

I was very surprised, pleasantly, when I received them. I had done extremely well. I was offered (and I accepted) a position with the Georgetown Law Journal, for which only the best students were eligible. I had achieved my goal that first year of law school.[1]

During my second year I was offered the position of

---

[1] All law schools have a Law Review or Law Journal for their best students, which publish books consisting of articles written by the student members of the Law Journal or outside legal scholars. Most of the top law firms only hire the student members of a Law Journal as associate attorneys, and Judges also only hire these same students as law clerks for a year or two.

Articles Editor of the Law Journal for my third year. That meant I would be one of seven members of the Executive Board of the Law Journal which ran it. That job involved editing the articles which we accepted from outside legal scholars for publication in the Law Journal, and I interacted with the authors regarding their articles. That was hard work, and I enjoyed it.

Here I was a star student at Georgetown Law and the Articles Editor of the Law Journal. I had achieved. I was an important person again. And all of this occurred in our Nation's Capital, Washington, D.C.

My third year of law school was also momentous in certain other respects. I did not have the money to pay the tuition and living expenses my third year (which my Dad had paid my first two years), and my Dad didn't want to pay for another year. It was time, he felt, for me to be self-sufficient and to support myself financially. But, he did give me the balance of the tuition money I had saved him at Tulane (after subtracting the amounts he had paid for my first two years of law school) to pay for everything. That was very generous of him, and it enabled me to pay for and finish law school. To help meet my living expenses, though, I would have to find a part-time job, and I did with one of the major D.C. law firms which paid me well to prepare legal research memoranda for them for their cases. So, on top of continuing to study hard for school, I was also working hard for the Law Journal as its Articles Editor (for which there was no pay) and working 15-25 hours a week on legal research projects for the law firm. I didn't get enough sleep during my third year.

As exams were approaching in May 1970 (my law school graduation year), other events occurred which helped me: (a) The United States invaded Cambodia as the war in Vietnam was still raging; (b) four students at Kent State College were shot and killed while protesting the Cambodian invasion; and (c) the anti-war and Civil Rights protests (which I supported) were getting worse and worse and threatening the domestic peace. Riots and looting occurred in D.C. and some other cities that Spring (which I did not support). While I was in the midst of studying for my final exams, the Georgetown Law Center announced that all exams for the students were postponed until August and that third-year students could receive administrative passes if they chose to graduate in May. I took the administrative passes and graduated. I was relieved not to have to study further for those final exams.

Those three years of law school were quite a ride for me, to put it mildly.

Plus, I had a great job lined up for the Fall: My one-year clerkship for Judge Fahy on the United States Court of Appeals for the D.C. Circuit, which I had applied for and was interviewed for by Judge Fahy. Judge Fahy had a highly distinguished career before he became a Judge, and I admired him greatly and was pleasantly surprised when he selected me for the clerkship. That judicial clerkship in D.C. was (and still is) considered by many as the best in the country except for a United States Supreme Court clerkship. During that clerkship year, I did apply for another clerkship on the Supreme Court, and was told I was a finalist for one with Chief Justice Warren Berger, but I didn't get it.

I had also learned during my third year of law school that if I took and passed the Louisiana Bar Exam, which is required to practice law in Louisiana, I could then also be waived into the D.C. Bar, on the basis that I was still domiciled in Louisiana as my permanent place to live and I had proof of that through my Louisiana Driver's License and my Louisiana Voter Registration. That killed two birds with one stone – entry into the Louisiana Bar and into the D.C. Bar too, if I ever actually practiced with a law firm in D.C. As things turned out, I did with Covington & Burling in D.C.

This plan also allowed me to return to New Orleans for the summer to take a Louisiana Bar Exam course, which I badly needed to do because Louisiana has the French Napoleonic Civil Code as its law rather than the Common Law which exists in every other state of the Country.[2] This plan also allowed me to move home for the summer to be pampered by my parents. My routine for about two months in New Orleans was to attend the Bar Review course five days a week from 6:00 p.m. to 10:00 p.m.; afterwards to study and learn the material at home until 5:00 a.m. to 6:00 a.m. the next morning; and then go to sleep until early afternoon. When I woke up my Mom would cook me brunch and an early dinner before the classes the next night. I wanted to learn the materials well for two reasons – first, to pass the exam and, second, to learn the materials if I ever returned to practice law. I did return five years later in 1975 when I was 30 years old.

The Good Years – Getting Married: Ages 26-30

My one-year clerkship with Judge Fahy on the United States Court of Appeals for the D.C. Circuit was a wonderful year for me, mixing with the other Judges' law clerks, some of the brightest minds in the United States.

Remember Abbie Hoffman, the renowned anti-war

---

[2] The Common Law is the law based on precedent of Court decisions, as developed over many decades, while the Civil Law is a Code of laws, but today they are mostly the same or very similar, because all the Common Law states have enacted the Uniform Commercial Code.

Hippie of the late 1960's who protested against the Vietnam War? He was arrested and convicted of a crime for wearing a shirt which resembled the American flag. That was actually a crime at the time. Judge Fahy dissented from the decision which upheld his conviction. I wrote the dissent for him on the basis that Mr. Hoffman was merely exercising his First Amendment free speech rights to protest.

I worked long hours that year, getting to work by 8:00 a.m. and often staying until 8:00 or 9:00 p.m. For legal research, I had access to the Court's substantial law library as well as the Library of Congress just a few blocks down the street, which had every book imaginable. I often checked the Records of the cases at hand when the arguments of counsel seemed wrong. I dug deep into the cases Judge Fahy was considering and wrote memoranda for him with my analysis and evaluation.

Judge Fahy told me that I had been the best law clerk he had ever had. That made me proud. He was an Irish Catholic and enjoyed our cultural differences, as did I. Up until that Judicial Clerkship year, I had always been a student.

After my year of the judicial clerkship with Judge Fahy I went to work as an associate attorney for Covington & Burling, which was and still is the top law firm in D.C. I stayed with Covington for four years and enjoyed working there a lot. It was and still is an amazing law firm. During my first year at Covington a book was published called the "Super Lawyers," and the entire first chapter of it was about Covington. I was proud to be part of that law firm and worked hard at my job.

More recently in 2018 another book was published about it, "Covington, A Centennial Story," which was written by Charles Miller ("Chuck" as we called him when I was there). Its uniqueness is shown in part by its various chapters, which include the following:

C&B on the World Stage – Europe
Covington on the World Stage – The Rest of the World

* * *

Food and Drug: Life Sciences
Communication/Media
Sports
Patents
International Trade and Investments
Foreign Governments/Projects
Government Contracts
Regulatory Regimes
Legislation/Public Policy

Covington often represented foreign governments regarding various and sundry matters. Attorneys there would often leave the firm for a few years to work in our Federal Government (at much lower pay) where they would acquire more expertise and national reputations, only to return to Covington afterwards. Covington represented the NFL, and years later the associate when I was there, Paul Tagliabue, who helped the partner in charge of the NFL work (and later became a partner), was selected as the Commissioner of the NFL. Covington also had former Secretaries of State, Attorneys General, and Senators among its partners, along with others who had been in high positions in our Federal Government. My best friend there, Jim, worked in the Antitrust Division of the Justice Department for a few years before returning to Covington.

I did work on some interesting matters at Covington. The firm represented the National Trust for Historic Preservation, which is a privately funded non-profit organization to help preserve America's own historic buildings. The well-known Willard Hotel, which is just a few blocks from the White House, was threatened to be demolished by real estate developers, and through Covington's involvement representing the National Trust, and through me primarily, it was saved. Today it is considered one of the finest and best, if not the finest and best, hotel in D.C., just as it was in the 19th Century. I also did legal work for the well-known Smithsonian Institute in D.C. regarding investment issues it was facing at the time. Dean Acheson, a former United States Secretary of State and a former Covington partner, died while I was with Covington, and I devised an aggressive tax plan for his Estate. In short, I worked on mostly high-profile, interesting matters while with Covington and enjoyed my years there a lot.

Again, being at Covington made me feel proud.

I met Sherrie in New Orleans for Thanksgiving in 1971, and we got married June 4, 1972 during my first year at Covington. I was one day shy of being 27, and Sherrie was 22. The marriage has worked well for both of us. Actually, I had met Sherrie previously at my brother Carl's wedding in Mississippi when I was 15 and she was 10, but we were both too young for any attraction.

While I was in D.C. working at Covington my Mom called and said I should ask Sherrie Burstein (who is Jewish) for a date over Thanksgiving while in New Orleans. My Mom and Dad were concerned that I hardly ever dated Jewish girls; as my Mom told me, there are cute Jewish girls too; she also reminded me that the cute girls get married young and I was getting older. She said Sherrie was cute, and I should ask Carl if I wanted confirmation. Carl confirmed she was cute and his wife, Sylvia, was extremely cute with a lot of personality. His recommendation carried a lot of weight with me.

Another connection between Sherrie and me is that her mother was Sylvia's oldest sister. That meant Sylvia was Sherrie's aunt and Carl was her uncle. That also meant that after we were married, Carl was also Sherrie's brother-in-law. Sylvia and Sherrie were very close growing up in Mississippi, and Sylvia was like an older sister for Sherrie. They both grew up in Moorhead, Mississippi, the tiny town where our Christmas tradition began with Sylvia's parents (and Sherrie's grandparents).

Another connection is that Carl's best friend at Tulane was Maury, who was Sylvia's older brother. Maury had invited Carl to Moorhead for Thanksgiving their first year of college, and when Carl got home afterwards all he could talk about was Maury's sister, Sylvia.

Of course, I met Sherrie years later over Thanksgiving too in New Orleans.

Our courtship was brief. She was living in New Orleans, and we saw each other every two weeks for weekends for seven weeks. On January 15, 1972, we got engaged. The reason, truth be told, is that I was insisting she move to D.C. to live, because I wanted to get to know her better before marrying her, and she was resisting moving unless we got engaged. So I figured, what the hell, let's get engaged, and I would refuse to set a wedding date until we both could be more certain we were compatible and wanted to be married.

Sherrie's parents were old-fashioned, and Sherrie never told them we would be living together in D.C. We rented an apartment for her in D.C. as "show" for them, but we never set foot in it. Those were the times back then.

I remember well that Thanksgiving Day in 1971 when

I picked Sherrie up at her parents' home. She was really attractive, had a lot of personality, and was short like me. Later that day (before the Thanksgiving meal with my parents) she pulled out a Tareyton cigarette to smoke; I had taken up smoking and liked Tareyton's the best too. As we drove around the City, we went to Cafe du Monde for coffee and beignets (donuts) and then to the Fly (in Audubon Park next to the Mississippi River) to talk and to get to know each other better. I kissed her and said, "you realize we'll probably get married one day." She replied, cutely, "when?"

Sherrie was raised in Moorhead, Mississippi and in the small town Indianola close by. My Mom was also raised in a small town in Mississippi. When I asked her once when younger what kind of girl I should marry, she replied, "a country girl" who is Jewish and who "loved me more than anything else in the World." Sherrie certainly met those specifications. She was very much like Sylvia, Carl's wife.

I also remember well Sherrie's first trip to D.C. to visit me two weeks after Thanksgiving. It was a Friday. When I came home from work to my apartment, she had cleaned it and cooked us a gourmet meal for dinner. During that dinner I remember thinking, "I really do need to marry this girl."

By age 26 I had already figured out the ideal spouse for me: Jewish if possible; very cute with a lot of personality; strong but not a career woman who might compete with me; and someone who adored me, and I her.

She certainly met all of my expectations.

I recall my parents were in D.C. in early April for a stop-over during one of their trips, and we met them for brunch. At brunch my Mom asked, "when are y'all getting married?" I replied, "we're not setting a date yet." She replied, "I'm not leaving D.C. until y'all set a date." I figured the best thing to do was to set a date far enough in the future that I would, by then, be certain I wanted to marry Sherrie. We were enjoying being engaged; why rush things. I suggested late August for a wedding date. My Mom resisted, "it's too hot in August in New Orleans." She also ruled out July for other but similar reasons. As we worked toward a date, I suggested late June. They had conflicts, my Mom said. Since June 4 would be the day before my birthday, we settled on June 11. They left D.C. later that day.

As Sherrie's Mom started planning the wedding for June 11, the hotel she selected was not available that date, but it was available June 4. When I resisted, everyone piled on to persuade me of June 4. I relented. By then it was clear I had lost any control over our wedding date.

We went to St. Thomas for our honeymoon. That was a fun time for us.

To say that my parents and Sherrie's parents were ecstatic that we got married is a gross understatement. To say that they were all very concerned about the spouse each of us might marry is also an understatement. They were beyond happy that we had found each other.

When I was a few months shy of turning 29, in 1974, I started thinking to myself: I'll be 29 soon, and then 30, and is this life in D.C. working at Covington what I want for the duration? Living in D.C. (or its suburbs) was fun and exciting and so was working at Covington, but did I want to raise children in D.C. where none of our parents and relatives lived? Would D.C. ever feel like home for me? Did I want the life of a Covington partner? The answers, I would learn months later, were no.

I recall being in New Orleans for Christmas that year, staying with my parents, when the local newspaper in the sports section compared a local player to me. I said to Sherrie, "they still remember me." As Sherrie would later say, I was just another fish in the big pond of D.C., but in New Orleans I would be a big fish in a smaller pond. That rang true for me as I thought about moving back to New Orleans.

I started applying for jobs in New Orleans. I received lots of offers, and I accepted one of them. By June 1975 when I turned 30, we had returned to New Orleans to live. Coincidentally, Mr. Lemle of my new firm, Lemle & Kelleher, was the Chairman of the Board of Newman when I graduated 12 years earlier and gave me my diploma at the graduation ceremony.

One other factor closed the deal for us: Sherrie became pregnant that Spring of 1975. We had two sets of parents and lots of cousins living in New Orleans. We were also fortunate that New Orleans was a very "cool" city in which to live. It still is.

We did set some ground rules with our parents: We wanted to be left alone mostly; we did not want regularly scheduled or weekly meals together; and we wanted our own space. They understood and were so ecstatic we moved home to New Orleans that they abided by our rules.

I guess we had become the adults and could set the rules now!

As you can tell, I was not a "hippie" or a "flower child" of the 1960's and the early 1970's (as portrayed in the movies "Woodstock" and "Hair"), as many of my age had become. My generation, I would say, were mostly against the War in Vietnam and were mostly in favor of the Civil Rights Movement for Blacks. In D.C. when there were protests against the War or in favor of Civil Rights, I would try to attend them in support of my own views too. I am proud to be a part of that generation which changed America forever, but I was not an activist; I was just a supporter. My life view at the time was that I had to take care of me, not the world, and I did that by attending law school and doing well, by working hard during my judicial clerkship year, and by working hard at Covington too.

And, I was certainly enjoying my life, especially after I met Sherrie.

Sherrie & Alan - After wedding

The Better Years – Returning to New Orleans and Children: Ages 30-40

I enjoyed turning 30. I felt it gave me more credibility as an attorney. Who wants a 20-something year old attorney? Returning home to New Orleans felt good.

We initially rented a townhouse in a nearby suburb of New Orleans (Lakewood North); a year or so later, we bought our first home in the same neighborhood; and three years later we found our dream home in another nearby suburb of New Orleans (Lakewood South). That was the home that flooded from Katrina.

The Jewish Country Club in New Orleans was called Lakewood. Yes, there was a Jewish Country Club for golfers, and it also had places to eat and socialize, a swimming pool, and tennis courts. We were members, and I would spend summer days there as a child. When the local Interstate, I-10, was constructed in the late 1960's (while I was away in D.C.), it was built to go through Lakewood Country Club, and the areas bordering I-10 were called Lakewood North (on one side of I-10) and Lakewood South (on the other side). Homes were built on what was the golf course which were more modern than the older uptown homes.

We also had our first child, Tiffany, that Fall of 1975. In Judaism the tradition is to name the child after a recently deceased close relative, who in our case was Sherrie's maternal grandmother, Fanny Klumok. We didn't like any of the "F" names, though. Tiffany had "Fanny" in it, and we honored Fanny in our own way.

Did I ever love Tiffany!! I had never experienced that depth of love for anyone. After I changed her dirty diaper a few times and got shit under my nails, I realized there was no one else in the world I would do that for and not dislike it. I told Sherrie that must be "true love."

Our second child, Allison, was born 3 ¼ years later. I adored and loved her just as much, and I remain very close to both Tiff and Ali (as we called them). They are very different in many ways; some would call Tiff Sherrie's child and Ali mine; and like Sherrie and me, Tiff and Ali are very close with each other. Our "Yo 4" (as I called us) times together were very special, and we enjoyed dinners out together and family vacations.

I enjoyed practicing law with my new firm in New Orleans, Lemle & Kelleher ("Lemle"), more than I had with Covington in D.C. I came to know the clients for whom I did work and interacted with them a lot. After a year I became a partner, which means I became a part owner of the firm. Eventually I worked my way up to the firm's Management Committee, and then Vice-Chairman of the firm, and then Co-Chairman. The firm made good money, as did I. It also had a lot of politics internally which were stressful.

During my 30's at Lemle (and thereafter) I worked on some interesting matters. The New Orleans law firms did (and still do) a lot of Admiralty (or Maritime) legal work for three industries in particular – first, the work generated by the barge lines and tankers traveling the Mississippi River; second, the companies that owned and operated vessels and other equipment that supported the offshore oil and gas exploration and development in the Gulf of Mexico; and third, the shipbuilders in and around the New Orleans area. These industries were booming in the 70's, 80's and 90's in particular. I became the business lawyer for the maritime clients of the firm.

I recall one case for a shipyard which had sold patrol boats to the Taiwanese Government; the patrol boats did not go as fast as they were required in order to catch smugglers and the like; and the shipyard was sued in New Orleans. I was asked to go to Taiwan with a client representative for a week to try to settle the case. At the negotiating sessions, Taiwan would have about 15 individuals present and they seemed to disagree among themselves a lot as they spoke Chinese. I led our negotiating team of two. It was a grueling week, and we settled the matter for a fraction of the authority the shipyard had given us to settle.

There were a lot of other interesting matters I worked on at Lemle for the 36 years I worked there.

Tiffany and Allison attended Newman School starting in kindergarten and graduated from it. That was my high school too, and I enjoyed being a parent of students there. They did well academically. Later Dustin and Brittany attended Newman too and also did well academically. Interestingly, we had children attending Newman for 30 consecutive years, which we've been told is the longest in the history of Newman.

My basketball days helped me in both D.C. and New Orleans. In D.C., Covington had a team which competed in a Lawyers League. Our center was Paul Tagliabue, then an associate like me, who went on to become the NFL Commissioner, as mentioned previously. I was probably the only person in New Orleans who was rooting for Paul at the time, since his competition was the former General Manager of our New Orleans Saints. Paul and I had become friends.

About a month after Katrina, I e-mailed Paul a few times to warn him that the owner of the Saints was planning to move the team to San Antonio permanently – where he had substantial business interests and where the Saints played their home games in 2005 after Katrina – and to explain how devastating that would be for New Orleans. He heard me (as he later acknowledged in person), and I probably had a hand in influencing Paul to stop any move by the Saints to another city during those times. Recall our Lt. Governor's explanation about what the Saints' first game in the Superdome meant for him, a devout Catholic: "The Resurrection of the City."

In New Orleans, there was a Lawyer's Basketball Tournament every year, and our firm had a team. We won one time on my last second shot from way out.

Our society looks up to athletes, probably more than warranted, and attorneys are no different. The fact that I had played college basketball in the SEC was something that others admired. That, plus my smarts, drive and hard work, and a decent personality, combined to help me be successful practicing law.

I also played a lot of tennis during those years. Recall that I had been City Champion for my age bracket when I was 15. Our Managing Partner during these years played tennis too, and we were competitive when we played. That probably helped me too.

Soon after returning to New Orleans, I was invited to be on the Regional Board of Directors of the Anti-Defamation League, also known as ADL, for its office in New Orleans which covered the South region of the United States. I accepted. ADL is a national non-profit organization whose mission is to combat Antisemitism and discrimination of all kinds in our Country and worldwide. After about eight years of serving on the Board, I was asked to be the Chairman of the Board. I accepted. It was a four-year term. ADL had an annual fundraiser, the Torch of Liberty Award Dinner, which grew in attendance over the years to 500-600 people. Only about half of the attendees were Jewish. The Chairman served as the Master of Ceremonies for the dinner. That gave me wide exposure around the City, which no doubt helped me to maintain a high profile in New Orleans and to be attractive to some as their attorney if they needed one.

The Executive Director of ADL's New Orleans office (its hired professional) was A.I. Botnick, who went by B. He did most of the work for ADL, not me. My relationship with him was close and he helped me to embrace my Judaism. Up until then I was always Jewish but not religious, and I didn't embrace being Jewish. For me I was Jewish religiously, and an American just making my way forward in the world like everyone else. My ADL involvement led to my enjoying being Jewish for perhaps the first time ever, and I have remained enjoying being Jewish as a parent of Jewish children and as a member of the New Orleans community.

I also started attending the national meetings of ADL in New York, Washington, D.C. (my old stomping grounds), and other cities. I found those meetings enriching personally. Here I was mixing with all the other ADL supporters and professionals in a meaningful way to try to combat Antisemitism and other types of discrimination in the Country.

After some years I was asked to be a member of ADL's National Board (called the National Commission); later I was asked to be a member of ADL's National Civil Rights Committee; and later to be the Vice-Chairman of its National Legal Affairs Committee. All of my ADL involvement, locally and nationally, consumed a lot of my time. But, I enjoyed the time commitment and became enriched through it.

On reflection, I frankly don't know how I was able physically and emotionally to take on so much: Being a full-time attorney practicing law hard; being so involved with ADL; exercising regularly; and raising my children and being with them a lot too.

When I was 36 years old I recall feeling "burnt out" from working so hard. I had been pushing hard in all phases of my life, including practicing law hard, playing sports hard, being so involved with ADL, being a parent and trying to spend time with my young children, and being social with clients and friends. I told Sherrie we should take a long vacation somewhere nice, and she agreed. My goal on this vacation would be to become bored, just as I had as a child during long hot summers in New Orleans. I wanted to experience a bit of boredom again. I had not experienced any since I was a young child.

We took a car trip for five weeks in our station wagon to Martha's Vineyard in Massachusetts. Tiffany was 5 and Allison was 2 ½ years old. Our first stop was in Chattanooga. We stayed in a railroad car at the Chattanooga Choo-Choo, which was fun, and we saw the sites the next day. We stopped in D.C. to show Tiffany and Allison the sites there. And we eventually made it to Martha's Vineyard, where we rented the house of a partner at Covington for a month.

We rented bicycles and enjoyed the four of us being together full-time. That made us closer than ever, which was special. I read the Bible for the first time ever; I always thought it would be interesting to read the most popular book in the World. After reading the Old Testament, I decided to read the New Testament. I also took up jogging for the first time, and years later ran a Marathon (26.2 miles). I sure enjoyed that family vacation, and I had indeed become bored.

In fact, after that family vacation we started taking summer vacations every year with our children for two to three weeks, including to Martha's Vineyard again, to Maine in different areas, to Wyoming and Colorado in different places, to Minnesota, to New York City, and to California in different places. During them we were with our children 24/7, and we enjoyed being together just us and getting to know each other better. I recall asking Tiff and Ali after that first vacation to Martha's Vineyard whether they like me better after the trip than before it, and they said after it. I think

I liked (loved) my children even more after each of those vacations too. They were very special for all of us.

During my 30's and 40's I also experienced watching my Mom deteriorate gradually from Alzheimer's over a 17-year period.

That was awful. My Mom had been the rock of my world – she adored me, and I her. She was the one who usually ruled the household. When my Dad became too strict with me, which he did at times, she would intercede and soften the situation. She was a great Mom, I always felt, and she always looked out for me. It was also sad that Sherrie, Tiffany, and Allison never got to spend quality time with my Mom, and she with them, during those years.

But, my true love had changed to Sherrie, and then our children, around the time my Mom was diagnosed with Alzheimer's. We had moved back to New Orleans by then. The real burden of my Mom becoming ill was my Dad's, not mine. I was lucky in this regard.

My Dad took good care of my Mom. He kept her at home for years because he enjoyed being with her so much. After a few years he hired sitters to stay with her during the day. But one day she left the apartment where they lived unbeknownst to my Dad or the sitter. No one knew where she went. We helped my Dad try to find her, but to no avail. He had friends looking too.

Later that day my Dad's friend found her at the City jail. Apparently, she was arrested for shoplifting in a nearby store. My Dad went to the jail and retrieved her.

After that my Dad decided it was time to put her in a nursing home. I recall the timing well, because Sherrie, Tiffany, Allison and I were set to leave for our wonderful vacation in Martha's Vineyard that same week. Sherrie's Dad also suffered a mild heart attack at the time. My goodness, what a situation! We did not leave on that vacation until a week later, after we were comfortable that Sherrie's Dad was okay and that my Mom had been settled in the nursing home and my Dad was okay.

After my Mom was in the nursing home my Dad visited her every day. How sweet of him to do that, I have always thought. But he did that for himself as much as for her; he enjoyed just being with her; and she no doubt enjoyed his presence too.

I visited my Mom in the nursing home regularly when I could, often with Tiffany and Allison. At first, I enjoyed seeing her. So did Sherrie. But as she started to deteriorate we went less often, because it was clear she did not even recognize us. Towards the last few years my visits became fewer, but I always went to visit her on her birthday, her anniversary, and Mother's Day.

It would upset me for days afterwards when I visited her. That was my problem, of course, but just as I avoided driving through the ruins of the City after Katrina because that upset me for days afterwards, I started finding excuses not to visit my Mom except for her birthday, anniversary, and Mother's Day.

My Dad complained that I didn't go visit her more. When I explained to him why, he seemed to understand and accept my reasons, but he clearly didn't like them. He continued to go visit her every day until she died.

When Sherrie learned that my Mom died, she called me at my office and suggested I go to the nursing home to meet my Dad who was going there too. I did. I recall walking into her room with my Dad, and he proceeded to close her eyes and kissed her for the last time. I kissed her too. I spent that day with my Dad.

I was very upset for weeks afterwards. My Mom, my

beloved Mom, had died. While she may have left us years earlier, she had not died.

When some of her or my Dad's friends said "it was for the best," I resented it. This was my Mom. And now she was gone forever, buried in the ground.

I still go visit the cemetery occasionally, where my Mom and Dad are buried next to each other. They were good parents.

The Even Better Years – And More Children: Ages 40-49

We had a party at our house for my 40th birthday!

Turning 40 meant I was middle-aged. I didn't like the concept or the fact – I was still living like I was 25 or 30. I recall Sherrie telling me that maybe I should stop exercising so hard and stop acting like a 25-year old still.

My idea of fun was to exercise to excess. In tennis, I preferred singles and would play hard for 2-3 hours straight in our summer heat and humidity. Jogging 6-10 miles was also intense.

At age 42, I hurt my back badly from carrying a heavy trial briefcase through airports while on business. Stupidly, I "played through" that injury, as I had always tried to do with sports injuries. A bad back is not an injury one should "play through." It was months later that I realized I needed to seek medical help for my back.

Even today at age 79, I struggle with my bad back. While I have been limited physically by my bad back, my brain still works well. Even with my bad back, I still walk 1 ½ miles briskly three times a week and do light weights once a week.

When I was 45 Sherrie became pregnant. We had

decided that we wanted more children, but she had had four miscarriages during the prior few years, and we had pretty much given up about having more children and had become blaze' about birth control. After those miscarriages, Sherrie went to a different doctor who helped her avoid any more miscarriages. Sherrie was 40 and I was 45 when Dustin (our son) was born.

On Sherrie's 40th birthday in April of that year she stayed home to rest due to being pregnant. I'm a terrible gift giver, and my practice was not to give her presents because she always complained about whatever I got her. She would instead just buy her own presents, and I would pay for them. She preferred that, it seems, given my bad gift giving over the years. Well, for her 40th birthday, I bought 40 gifts for her and gave them to her during the course of the day. One was a coffee mug which said "I'd rather be 40 than pregnant." None of the gifts were extravagant, and she enjoyed her 40th birthday at home being pregnant with me.

We were happy to have a son, Dustin. Almost two years later, Sherrie became pregnant again and had Brittany. When Brittany was born, Tiffany was almost 17, Allison was 13, and Dustin was almost 2. During the C-section delivery we asked the Doctor to "tie Sherrie's tubes" to avoid more pregnancies. When I reminded the doctor twice during the delivery to tie her tubes he said to everyone in the operating room, "does anyone think I'll forget to tie her tubes." I was 47 and Sherrie 42 when Brittany was born.

Having Dustin and Brittany, and now four children, was a real blessing for us. We apparently have been good at raising our children, and we enjoyed having the full household. The older two adored their younger brother and sister (and each other too), and the younger two of course adored their older sisters.

Our four children have remained close with each other and with us. We call the six of us "Yo Fam," and the six of us have a Yo Fam group text, as it is called, where we communicate something with each other almost daily, and often about 25 times or more a week. Tiffany has five children of her own; Allison has two; and Brittany has one but is expecting a second. Dustin is recently married.

I would imagine that our having those last two children became a hot topic of conversation among our friends with the typical conversation going something like this: "Can you believe what the Goodmans have done?" "I'm sure glad it's them and not us." "They're really crazy, don't you think?" But we didn't care and enjoyed our life even more, as our Yo Fam continued to grow with spouses and grandchildren. It's fun to have a large family when there's a lot of love.

One of the nicest things ever for us also occurred when I was 44. One of my ADL colleagues locally (Allan Katz) wanted to write an article about the Jews of New Orleans. He asked me if I would mind if he made my family the focus of the article, because my family had been in New Orleans for four generations. I said sure.

The title of his article became "The Journey of Abraham." My paternal grandfather was named Abraham (as was the first patriarch of Judaism), and my family of four at the time was featured in the article, including pictures of us. The article was published in New Orleans Magazine, a local monthly magazine, and was read widely in the City.

Some portions of the article which I think readers will find interesting, educational, and enjoyable are the following:

> As with all immigrant groups, the story of
> the Jews of New Orleans is a tale of long

journeys to America and the planting of roots.

Among the beneficiaries of one of those long journeys is Alan Goodman, today a partner in the old-line New Orleans law firm of Lemle and Kelleher.

Alan Goodman starts his daily journey with a kiss for his wife of 18 years, Sherrie, and a ride from his Lakeview home first to Uptown New Orleans to drop off Tiffany, 14, and Allison, 11, at Newman School, then downtown to his office on Poydras Street where he runs the law firm's commercial section.

But the journey of Abraham and Ethyl Goodman, his paternal grandparents, was not quite so pleasant. They were born and grew up in the Russia of the czars in the late 19th century. The Goodmans lived in The Pale, a brutally cold, desolate slice of land sometimes controlled by Russia and sometimes by Poland. It was a hard way of life many Americans have come to know something of through the stage play and movie, "Fiddler On The Roof." At that time, it was the only place that Jews could legally live in either Russia or Poland and there were oppressive, racist laws to limit their education and the ways they could earn a living. It was not a land of milk and honey.

In 1881, life in The Pale became unbearable and intolerable for the Jews under Czar Alexander III. Thousands of Jews died in anti-Semitic riots, and hundreds of thousands were conscripted to serve in the czar's armies where they died as cannon fodder in his wars. The noose of oppression finally became so unbearable that the bravest left The Pale, many dreaming of a faraway paradise they'd heard of called America.

"Fiddler On The Roof" ends with the Jews leaving their village in The Pale as it burns behind them. Actually, that was only the beginning of the trip. The next stop was Hamburg, in Germany, 500 miles away. There were only two ways for Jews to get to Hamburg from The Pale, on foot, or, for the lucky ones, on a wagon drawn by oxen or mules.

In Hamburg, the Jews worked where they could to earn money for a steerage class passage to a British seaport, like Liverpool. Once in Liverpool, they again worked wherever they could earn passage for another trip in steerage, this time to the promised land of America.

The Goodmans came to New Orleans. They came here because a relative from The Pale had come here earlier. They couldn't speak English and had nothing but the clothes on their backs but they wanted to come to a place where they would know someone who might understand their fears, aspirations and concerns.

This explanation about the hard times and the difficulty to get to America was very illuminating, I thought. Indeed, as my Dad later told me, his oldest sister (Rose) was born in Russia, and my Dad's mother (Ethyl) and Rose came to America first. It was some years later before his dad (Abraham) was able to join them in New Orleans, after which they had four more children. My Dad, Ben, was the youngest. When I was a child, my Dad would take me to visit his mom (Ethyl), who was Bubbie to me, as well as one of her brothers who came here too. As my Dad explained in the article about his upbringing:

"My parents never talked about where they lived in The Pale, the name of the town where they resided or how they got out," recalls Ben Goodman, the youngest of the five children born to Abraham and Ethyl in New Orleans. "My parents were American patriots. Rather than talk about the Old Country, they talked to their children about the New Country, the opportunities we had here, the freedom…. They knew in a way that their children, grandchildren or great-grandchildren would never understand how lucky they were to be in America. It took my father nearly 20 years to master his English well enough so that he could read the daily paper from cover to cover, and that is what he did every day – he read it with pride and pleasure. Perhaps it was his way of celebrating the trip out of The Pale that he wouldn't discuss."

Because Abraham Goodman had no way of earning a living in New Orleans, he first became a peddler. He would buy simple goods on credit – ranging from pots and pans to second-hand clothing – and pile it on a cart that he would take through New Orleans neighborhoods, learning English and French phrases on the street, building his vocabulary and, on good days, selling his goods at a profit.

He did well enough that by the 1900s, he was in the scrap business, trading in pieces of steel and metal that had been discarded or sold at the cheapest rates. It was not a business for a man concerned with keeping his fingernails clean, but Abraham Goodman was more interested in feeding his wife and his five Jewish-American children.

In the early years, like the other Jewish immigrants from Eastern Europe during that time, the Goodmans lived in a small apartment on South Rampart Street. But as Abraham did better, he was able to buy a once-elaborate mansion fallen on hard times with ten rooms on Carondelet Street near Jackson Avenue. He made six rooms into apartment units and turned the other four rooms into his own apartment.

Abraham and Ethyl Goodman initially worshipped God in New Orleans in much the same way they had in Eastern Europe. As soon as they could, they joined two Orthodox Jewish congregations (they joined two because it meant more social contacts and business opportunities) – Anshe Sfard on Carondelet Street and Beth Israel, then on Carondelet Street and Euterpe near St. Charles Avenue. The Beth Israel congregation has since moved to Canal Boulevard.

At these Orthodox congregations, the prayers were recited in Hebrew, the conversations were a mixture of English and Yiddish and the women were seated separately from the men, following the teachings of the Old Testament.

Interestingly, that was not the way most Jews in New Orleans prayed to God, then or now. Unwittingly, the Goodmans had come to one of the oldest Jewish communities in America, already steeped in American traditions, distinguished and wealthy. The overwhelming majority of Jews in this established community practiced Reform Judaism where both the prayers and conversations were mostly in English, where organ music accompanied the religious service and where men and women sat together. This was no accident. The Reform Jews wanted their religious services to closely resemble a Christian church service. It was, says Rabbi Cohn, "a way of binding and incorporating themselves to the majority Christian community. The Reform Jews wanted their own identity, but they did not want to be so markedly different that they could not participate in the larger community."

I love this explanation about my Dad's parents and the times they endured seeking a better life for themselves and their children. They were always looking ahead seeking a better life, just as my parents did for themselves and for their children, and just as we have done for ourselves and our children. The author then explains:

The arrival of the Eastern European Jews in New Orleans during the period from 1870-1900 caused some problems, as surges of immigrants often do.

During that 30-year period, many of New Orleans' leading luncheon clubs and Mardi Gras krewes reacted to the arrival of a wave of Jewish immigrants by adopting by-laws that barred entry to any but Christians. It is a ban that exists today and is a source of irritation for some New Orleans Jews, although it is less a cause of concern for

Jewish leaders than it once was as new, open Mardi Gras krewes and luncheon clubs have emerged here. It is a point to ponder that the first Rex was Louis Solomon, a leading Jewish businessman, but there has been no Jewish Rex since.

I never felt the sting of these exclusionary clubs (which sponsored many of the Mardi Gras parades, debutante parties, and the like) and never wanted any of that for myself. After all, we had our own exclusionary customs, including Bar (and Bat) Mitzvahs and our own Country Club. I have always enjoyed Mardi Gras, though. The author further writes:

> By 1940, Abraham and Ethyl Goodman had entered the final phase of their lives and could look back with satisfaction at their achievements. They had escaped The Pale and the clouds of World War II and the Holocaust that now hovered over Europe and its helpless Jews. Their five children had received an American education and had begun promising careers. Although never wealthy, the Goodmans had prospered in America.

> Ben Goodman, the youngest of the five children of Abraham and Ethyl, married Sally Carp, also a second generation American Jew, in the midst of the Great Depression in 1935. A public school graduate, Ben gained undergraduate and law degrees from Tulane University, but it was a tough time for young

lawyers to make a living. Later, he drifted into the auto financing business where he earned a comfortable middle-class living.

In the 1940s, Ben and Sally left the Orthodox congregations where their parents worshipped and changed their affiliation to Touro Synagogue. In a short time, they were comfortable with the rituals of Reform Judaism. Their children attended Touro Synagogue through their growing up years and today their grandchildren attend services there.

But Sally Carp Goodman dreamed of something more for her three children, Carl, Malcolm and Alan. For starters, she wanted the best education for them that money could buy in New Orleans. So the Goodmans did without vacations and kept the family car an extra year or two so her sons could attend Newman, the city's most expensive, competitive prep school.

My Mom's parents, Ida and Charles Carp, lived in New Orleans too, along with two of my Mom's three sisters. I remember well the Passover Seders (a big meal with wine and a service) at the Carp's modest home; I was the youngest of all of my first cousins on my Mom's side of our family. I always enjoyed those Seders a lot. I also recall when Ida's (my maternal grandmother's) sisters would visit from Mexico where they lived; they had been unable to come to America from Russia (for reasons never explained to me) and immigrated to Mexico instead. They spoke no English, and my parents conversed with them in Yiddish while I conversed in Spanish (which I learned at Newman). And, as the author writes about this Alan guy:

> Alan Goodman recalls of his Newman years, "Although we were from a middle-class home, we were probably the poorest kids at Newman from a standpoint of wealth. But we were never intimidated by the opulence there because we were all blessed with good minds, athletic ability and a love of learning our mother had instilled in us. Those things made us feel the equals of everyone else. In that sense, Newman was a meritocracy. If you achieved, you could fit in, regardless of any economic differences."

> Alan Goodman says that in his home, not much was said about the sacrifices of his grandparents or his parents so that the third generation could go to Newman, in much the same way that the grandparents never spoke of their escape from The Pale. "But we knew," he remembers. "It wasn't something we had to talk about."

* * *

Alan turned out to be the best athlete – although he is only 5'7" and barely weighed 150 pounds dripping wet while in high school. He led two undefeated state championship basketball teams. He also was All-state. He quarterbacked the football team to an unbeaten season. It is a joke among his friends that nothing he has done in his life was as important as playing on state basketball championship teams. But what was even more important was that he finished second in his class at Newman.

* * *

He says now that one of the fundamental questions he grappled with during those years was the issue of his Jewishness. "We weren't a religious family in the sense of praying all the time or going to synagogue every day, but there was an awareness of what I think of as Jewish values in our home – a sense of Jewish identity, working hard and studying hard, feeling a real love of America and knowing how lucky we are to live in such a great place, aspiring to great things because we have the opportunity to achieve them here. I decided that I liked all of that."

After graduation from Georgetown, he was chosen for a position at the powerful Washington law firm of Covington and Burling. Known as one of the country's "super law firms," Covington and Burling attracted a lot of the best and brightest. On the firm's basketball team, Goodman was the point guard who fed the ball to a gangling attorney named Paul Tagliabue who played center. At the recent Super Bowl played in New Orleans, Tagliabue, now the commissioner of the National Football League, recalled Goodman as "the shortest guard I played with after I finished grammar school."

* * *

Although Goodman did well in Washington, he missed New Orleans. "I've always loved the city" he says. "I think New Orleans is the best place to live in the world. And I was really bothered in the late 1960s when my father had heart surgery and his sons were all living in other places. So I came home and got a job at Lemle & Kelleher."

He also found a wife. Sherrie Burstein was raised in Mississippi. Like her husband, she is a third-generation descendant of Jews who escaped The Pale. She grew up in the little town of Indianola where her family owned a department store. At that time, there were just 10 Jewish families in Indianola. She frequently visited Meridian where the Jewish community was a little larger.

* * *

The small Jewish community in Mississippi followed the tenets of their religion avidly. Sherrie Burstein's grandmother, Fanny

Davidson Klumok, was known as "the grand dame of the Delta" because she was so active in maintaining Jewish culture wherever Jewish families gathered around the state. She was often asked to address Mississippi church groups to explain Jewish culture and religion. The Bursteins and the Klumoks were Jews glad to be acculturated, but they didn't want to be assimilated and lose their Jewish identity.

Of their courtship, Goodman says: "I was looking for someone who would bring the same values to our home and to our children as my mother gave to my brothers and me. Sherrie and I had known each other as teenagers, but I hadn't paid much attention to her because she was five years younger. But when we met again as adults, it was clear to both of us that we shared the same values and the same view of the world. We were engaged seven weeks later."

Today, Sherrie Burstein Goodman is considered one of the top volunteers in New Orleans, working for the National Council of Jewish Women, the New Orleans Symphony, Newman School and the Jewish Federation. The National Council of Jewish Women has also been part of the fabric of New Orleans. A non-profit group, the NCJW sponsored pilot programs that led to the formation of the New Orleans Recreation Department, Head

Start, and a new pre-kindergarten education program for low-income students now being installed in many of the city's public schools.

This article certainly helped to establish us in the New Orleans community. I felt very honored. I learned a lot from the article about my own Dad and Mom and about their parents. Our forefathers did well for us in many ways, and Sherrie and I have aspired to do so well for our own children and for theirs. So far I think we have, and since they are all married and seemingly happy now, it may be that our job is done for them. But wait, what am I thinking? Our job with them is never done until the day we die, because we are role models for them forever!!

Something else very nice for me occurred just a few years later. During the years of my active ADL involvement, I was invited to go on an ADL Mission to Germany, which had only recently reunited East Germany with West Germany. There were about 30 of us on the Mission. The Berlin Wall separating West Berlin from East Berlin had been torn down. On that trip, we met with Germany's Chancellor and with other German political leaders in Bonn, the capital, and then we saw the rebuilt Berlin too. We learned a lot on that trip and felt good afterwards about Germany as a world leader which then, and today, is the second largest supporter of Israel after the United States.

After the trip I delivered a speech I had prepared about it to a National Meeting of the ADL and to a few local audiences. Some portions of it which I think readers will find interesting, educational, and even enjoyable are the following:

I had read in the newspapers about the right-wing violence in Germany – mostly against foreigners, but also the desecration of Jewish memorials and cemeteries. I surmised that Germany was probably experiencing little more than what we experience in America – right wing violence by neo-Nazi groups. Still, why was the German Government so slow to respond to the violence and to crack down on it?

★ ★ ★

Most importantly, did Germany recognize that it does have a higher moral responsibility due to its past than any other country in the world? We are entitled to measure Germany differently, by a different yardstick. Was Germany measuring up to this higher standard? That for me was a critical question.

So, when the Anti-Defamation League organized a mission to Germany to investigate the situation, I readily accepted the invitation to participate.

There were 30 of us participating in the Mission, including the National Chairman, the National Director, and the National Director of International Relations. We represented 22 different states. It was clear to the German Government that each of us would be reporting to our communities on the events in Germany.

The itinerary was intense. In 2 ½ days in Bonn, the capital of Germany, we met with Chancellor Kohl ....

Remember that Germany is the largest and strongest country economically in Europe and is an important ally of our Country, as is all of Europe. As I explained:

Germany is a country with its unique set of problems. It has 80 million people, the largest population in Europe. About 20 percent, or 16 million, come from the former East Germany. So, one-fifth of the German population for the past 47 years has grown up under a Communist regime – they have been educated differently about almost everything, including history and the Holocaust, and have been taught that the Government would provide for them. Imagine the culture shock – now, they had to provide for themselves, because the Government would no longer provide for them; things they had been taught about German history, and the horrors of the 1930's, were no longer true; and the youth now looked askance at their elders.

So, what has the German response been to the recent spate of right-wing violence against foreigners and the recent rise of neo-Nazism in a very small minority of the people?

Without exception, the German leaders expressed feelings of shame and grief over the recent right-wing violence. Foreign Minister Kinkel said, and I quote, that he was "ashamed" and that we are in fact entitled to measure Germany "by a different yardstick, and rightly so." ... As Kinkel said, we do have the right to watch Germany closer and to expect more from them. He recognized that "never again," to use his words, can Germany engage in violence against its minorities, including foreigners.

Germany has the most liberal asylum laws in the world. If you or I, or anyone else, were to show up at a German border and say, without more, that we seek asylum, we would automatically be accepted into the country, no questions asked, and would then be subject to a two to three-year process to determine whether we are entitled to asylum due to religious, ethnic or political persecution. We would also be provided with shelter and other financial support. In 1992, about 1.5 million foreigners, representing 70 percent of all European migration, moved to Germany seeking a better life. That is a tremendous burden for a country to absorb. Foreign Minister Kinkel stressed that Germany has done more in the field of human rights over the last few years than all of the rest of Europe combined. Yet, he was quick to add that the burden of accepting so many refugees was no excuse for the right-wing violence against foreigners.

* * *

So, it was clear that while Germany was slow to react aggressively against the violence, it has now recognized the problem, has mustered the will to deal with it, and is in fact now dealing with it effectively. Since late November 1992, when the efforts began in earnest, there have been fewer incidents against foreigners.

In short, I was most pleased to learn that Germany has evolved over my lifetime into a strong country with an especially close connection to the harm and horrors which can result from discrimination of all types. As I further explained:

> The highlight of the trip was our meeting with Chancellor Kohl. He stated unequivocally that the Jewish community in Germany is safe; that acts of anti-Semitism are barbaric; and that democracy in Germany is not at risk. He said, being frank, that the barbaric acts of the past are incomprehensible and that Germany can never adequately redress what happened to the millions and millions who were slaughtered but can only beg pardon. In his view the recent violence is linked not to anti-Semitism but, rather, to the millions of foreigners living in Germany,

but Germans have learned the lessons from the past. He believed that the vast majority of Germans want peace and freedom and abhor the violence, and he referred to the recent explosion of anger and shame in the mass candlelight demonstrations across Germany against the violence. Looking ahead, Chancellor Kohl advocated a United States of Europe, recognized the enormous difficulties in accomplishing this, but is optimistic that it will happen one day. That Kohl scheduled an entire 60 minutes for our meeting, and then stayed with us for a full 1 1/2 hours, showed his sense of importance for our Mission.

So, we have in Germany a country facing its two biggest challenges since 1945 – first, dealing with the German unification which occurred in October 1990; and, secondly, dealing with the totally new Europe and new world.

Did you know that Germany, second only to the United States, provides the most support for Israel, economically and politically, and sends the most visitors to Israel? According to the Israeli ambassador to Germany, a Holocaust survivor, Germany leads Europe in its support for Israel, and his hope is that Germany will persuade the rest of Europe to trade more openly with Israel and to follow the German opposition to the Arab boycott.

On a more personal note, the trip and my experiences from it were important to me. As I explained:

> For me, the trip was an emotional tug of war – a struggle between my stomach and head, between my emotional and rational sides. For all Americans, indeed for the entire world, and especially for Jews, it is so easy to hate the Germans. Visiting Sachsenhausen, a concentration camp, gripped me all over. Yet, the world moves forward, with or without us. Do we forever condemn Germany? Certainly, it is not fair to visit the sins of the parents on the children. And today, it is the children who now populate and run Germany. For the people of Germany, the children and grandchildren, it is difficult for them to be proud of their past – they admit that. The entire balance sheet of assets and liabilities must be considered by Germans when they measure their past, and the darkness does not overcome the good parts. I hope, and actually believe, that Germany will work hard to never forget its past and to always be sensitive to that past, even hundreds of years from now. For Jews, other minorities and the world, that would be good.

* * *

> One final point: Almost all of the political leaders we met were bright, sensitive,

reflective and candid. They certainly spoke to the issues. Many were women who showed a special sensitivity to the issues. In short, the German leaders we met were most impressive in their candor, sensitivity and intellect. Hopefully, they will meet the tasks ahead. It is our job to help them do so.

I think this trip and my speech about it, as well as the "Journey of Abraham" article, firmly established in the minds of others that I had become an important person in the City. This made me feel proud. I continued thereafter with my endeavors to be an "important person" in other ways too during my 40's.

For example, I served on Task Forces for Louisiana's then-elected Governor, Charles "Buddy" Roemer. I had become an avid supporter of him. But as Governor, I was disappointed over his performance during his administration.

I was also appointed to a Governor's Super Bowl Task Force for a Super Bowl to be held in New Orleans, which included a wonderful trip (with Sherrie) to Tempe, Arizona (a suburb of Phoenix) for the Super Bowl the prior year. I recall telling Paul Tagliabue, then the NFL Commissioner, that I would be there for the Super Bowl and suggesting we have dinner one night while there. He replied that he liked the idea but wasn't sure his schedule would allow for it. Little did I realize that Paul was like the president of a large country at the Super Bowl who would make brief appearances at various social events each evening but then leave after a short speech. It was not until years later when he had two occasions to be in New Orleans that we had dinner with our wives both times.

I also was invited and participated in our Mayor's Trade Mission to Japan (again, with Sherrie) in an effort to generate more business between Japan (whose economy was booming at the time) and New Orleans. Years later, I represented a major Japanese shipbuilder regarding its dispute with a major New Orleans shipbuilder. That representation was challenging but meaningful for me.

Sherrie and I also led a one-week Mission to Israel for about 30-40 of the younger leaders of the New Orleans Jewish Community. We had both been to Israel a couple of times previously, and we made a lot of new friends with younger couples during that trip. That was a memorable time for us. It also led to more legal work for me from some of the other participants.

I also attended the First Annual Meeting of Lex Mundi in Friebourg, Germany (again, with Sherrie). In this regard, I had become one of the six founders of Lex Mundi at the request of the person trying to create and organize it. Lex Mundi has become an organization of top law firms in every State of our Country and in every Country in the World, with each State and each other Country having one firm as its member. Lemle was the member for Louisiana. I had become enthusiastic that Lex Mundi would generate huge amounts of legal work for our law firm, and its annual meetings were always enjoyable events where I mixed with attorneys from other parts of the world and learned about their lives. For reasons which I never understood fully, Lex Mundi was not as profitable for Lemle (and its other member firms) as I had hoped it would be.

All of these things and travels were enjoyable for me and helped to raise my profile in the legal community, while I continued to work hard.

Sherrie & Alan

Dustin, Tiffany, Allison & Brittany December 1997

The Good Years Continue: Ages 50-59

They say 50 is "the youth of old age." I declared my birthday a personal holiday from work from that day forward. Allison spent my 50th birthday holiday with me. We played racquetball at a gym, and I beat her badly. She was pissed that I played so competitively, and I made no apologies. We laughed about it later that day.

During my 50's I was working harder and harder. When I told my Dad how hard I was working, he told me "this is your time -- you're in the prime of your career -- and you should be working hard to provide for your beautiful family." That seemed like good advice at the time. But I still managed to play sports and exercise a lot, because it helped me deal with my work stress better.

It was in my 50's that I also became an Adjunct Professor at Tulane Law School. Adjunct Professors are not paid at Tulane, and Tulane has to accept you as an Adjunct Professor. One of my ADL colleagues, Paul, taught at Tulane, and his specialty was bankruptcy. That was also one of mine, and he approached me about teaching a seminar with him about Chapter 11 Reorganizations. As he explained, he actually knew very little about Chapter 11 Reorganizations even though he taught the basic bankruptcy course at Tulane, but he knew how to teach and we would be a good team because he would lead the class and I would explain the Chapter 11 complex process. The only problem was that we had no book or other materials from which to teach about Chapter 11 Reorganizations, and we would have to create the materials for any course. Since he knew so little about the subject, as he explained, I would have to create the materials.

I did. I had recently completed a large, complicated

Chapter 11 Reorganization Case representing the Debtor and had been wildly successful with the result. I created the class materials from that case, and called the Debtor "Deadbeat," since every creditor regards the Debtor as a deadbeat, and called the major secured lender "Gorilla," since every Debtor regards its secured lender as an 800-pound gorilla. I created the topics for each week of the class with eight pre-plan topics, and then eight plan topics. Confirmation of a Chapter 11 Plan of Reorganization for the Debtor is the ultimate goal of all Chapter 11 cases, even today.

We had the students write memoranda on the selected topics for each class, and the students who wrote the memorandum for that week would teach the class, along with our help of course. According to Paul (the other professor) and some of the students' written evaluations of the course, it may have been the most difficult class at the law school, and it may also have been the best. Paul and I were active in helping the students understand the materials, including the different topics and the applicable law, and the students enjoyed learning it.

The course was taught once a week on Mondays from 5:00 p.m. to 7:30 p.m. As a result, on the weekends I would have to read the memoranda for that week and prepare for the class, which took about five hours on average. On Mondays I would have to leave the office early and got home late for dinner. During the rest of the week, I still practiced law hard.

I had always looked up to and admired my teachers and professors. When the students addressed me as Professor Goodman, I was surprised initially and smiled to myself that I was now a Professor at a law school.

I'm not sure how I managed to work so hard during my 50's. When I was 60 Katrina happened and I decided I would have to discontinue teaching afterwards due to so many other pressures during that time. As I would later say, teaching that course became a Katrina casualty.

It was during my 40's and 50's that I realized the keys to dealing with stress for me were the following: (a) a good night of sleep; (b) sex occasionally with my wife (I've never strayed); (c) lots of exercise regularly; (d) a good bowel movement in the morning; and (e) a good regular diet, including breakfast. Allow me those five things and I was ready to take on the world.

It was during this period when I also told my children that "boring is fun" when they complained that I would watch television in the evenings to try to relax. They laugh at me.

I also became a grandfather for the first time in my late 50's. Tiffany (and Mitchell, who we call Meshoo) had a boy Miles, and Tiff gave me the grandfather name "Cowboy Al" when we were at Malcolm's ranch in Texas after I dressed as a cowboy to ride a horse to help herd the cows. I am anything but a cowboy and was just having fun, but Tiff persisted in calling me Cowboy Al. When Miles later started talking around age 2, the words came out as "Ky," and to this day my grandfather name has remained Ky. It's a ridiculous grandfather name of course, but that became part of the fun for everyone calling me Ky. I embraced the name and the fun of being called Ky, and to this day everyone in the family calls me Ky as a nickname.

I also learned to enjoy Rap music in my 50's. Dustin and Brittany, our second generation of children who were much younger than Tiffany and Allison, listened to it. My favorites then were Nelly, 50 Cent and Eminem, and later Lil Wayne became my favorite. I like the music and beat, and also the lyrics which I found funny because they were often so outrageous. My cell phone ringtone is 50 Cent's "In da Club." My law partners laugh at me too.

But, I would still put our music of the 1960's as the best ever – The Beatles, The Rolling Stones, Bob Dylan (who was later awarded the Nobel Prize for poetry), Fats Domino, James Brown, and others.

I still listen to music when I drive to and from work. It brightens my day.

I've also tried my hand at poetry. At Tulane my Senior year I took a poetry class. When playing tennis with one of my best friends (John) I had trouble calling balls in or out because I had a stigmatism in my eyes which contact lens did not correct. John, who is not Jewish, complained about it to me in a letter from a fictitious law firm in a funny, hilarious way. I wish I had his letter to share. I replied with a Sonnet as my own funny reply, as follows:

> To respond or not to respond,
> That is the question.
> Tis better to bear knife marks in one's back,
> Than to sling arrows and mud back.
> But oh, how long can one's patience endure.
> Must we, in the course of life, never strike back.
> Are we only in this world for others to strike,
> And be there so they can take their shots.
> Woe is the lot of the Jewish athlete,
> Like his brother warriors in Israel,
> To fight back, or not to fight back,
> In either case, we lose.
> To respond or not to respond,
> That is the question.

John and I remain good friends. We have laughed about our exchanges over the years.

My only other Sonnet was to a female attorney (who is

now a partner) who was about to get married. I could tell she was having second thoughts about the whole marriage thing. My Sonnet to her read:

To marry or not to marry,
That is the question,
Whether tis better to bear the risks and burdens
Of a marriage, with so many emotional ups
and downs and possibly children too,
In order to experience marriage's joys and happiness too.
Do I prefer the merry-go-round of my
current life which nicely goes
Round and round and round, or
Would a roller-coaster ride which goes
up and down, up and down,
up and down, be better for me.
Woe is the lot of the career woman,
Who wants all in life there is to offer,
But with so much stress trying to do it all.
What is best for me?
Am I to be bold and adventuresome, and pursue it all,
Or cautious and careful so as not to
disturb my balance, equilibrium,
And well-being.
That is the question only I can answer.

She did get married and now has two children.

Truthfully and in my mind, nothing much during my 50's happened to us of any consequence other than we were leading the "good life." But in retrospect, we were doing a lot while leading the "good life."

Katrina and The Law Practice: Age 60-69

When I turned 60 all of my children came to or were already living in New Orleans and spent the day with me at home. There was nothing else I wanted to do that day except spend it with them. Tiffany, our family musician, put together an ensemble of Beatles songs but with lyrics suited for just me, and the four of them performed and sang them to me. The songs included Paperback Writer, Helter Skelter, I am the Walrus, and others, but with lyrics suited only for me. That was special!! I turned 60 in June 2005, and the floodwaters in our home a few months later from Katrina have destroyed those lyrics (there were no Google drives back then). I would have enjoyed sharing some of them here.

I was still working hard at the time. I recall thinking that I'm 60 years old and is this how I want to spend my 60's and the rest of my life? A few months later, August 29, Hurricane Katrina arrived. That certainly turned my life upside down, as I've already described.

Katrina represented a lot of new, unknown challenges for us. While I would in no way wish those or similar challenges on anyone else, or myself again, they did require me to "rise to the occasion" and to deal with everything. In the end, I survived admirably and remained strong mentally, emotionally, and physically.

A friend told me, what doesn't kill us makes us stronger. I'm not sure I agree but it sounds good.

As mentioned previously, natural disasters are good for the law business, and my law practice became more substantial as a result. I was doing well at work.

My law firm had an age rule at the time. When a partner turned 65, the traditional retirement age in our society, the partner was reduced in compensation by 10% each year until he/she reaches 70. That rule had never bothered me, because it had never affected me and it created opportunities for me. But after Katrina, while my law practice was doing so well, I came to realize I didn't like that rule. In today's world, and at that time too, a partner's compensation is based primarily on his/her production, meaning dollars produced.

The rule seemed to me to be antiquated, as well as discriminatory based on age for our firm to have that rule. I told that to all of the partners. I did not threaten to sue the firm if the rule was not changed, because that would have been harmful to my reputation, I figured. I also did not threaten to leave the firm if the rule was not changed, but I was certainly considering doing so. Everyone seemed to understand my sentiment and agreed with it.

At the vote to eliminate all age rules in the partnership articles which governed us, the result was unanimous. No more age rules would apply to us.

After that, I settled in at my firm and continued to work hard and do well.

About five years later, the law firm started having some subpar years. I recall that in 2009 we had a terrific year. In 2010, however, our revenues declined substantially, as did my compensation which was based on a percentage of the firm's profits. I was still producing at a high level, as were a few others. I stayed loyal to the firm through 2010, though, even as my income declined substantially and much more than was fair to me.

That next year, 2011, started slowly for us. I raised my concerns for the first time, including the need for us to start reducing our expenses and for non-productive partners to accept reductions in their compensation. There was heavy resistance to both. I continued to press forward for changes while others of us were still producing at high levels.

After a few months of this discussion, I realized I should start looking for other alternatives to my law firm. A major law firm in Baton Rouge, Louisiana (our State Capital) approached me to see if I was interested in joining it. I was 66 at the time. Was it crazy for me to be looking for a new firm at my age?

Such a lateral move to another law firm would no doubt be very stressful and challenging in ways I could not anticipate. My ultimate rationale in favor of the move was that if I was able to get through Katrina without damage to my mental and emotional well-being, then this move should be a "piece of cake," and the move made good sense in terms of money and stability. My feelings also told me this was the smart and best thing to do. A new challenge at age 66 was exciting for me in a way.

During the course of the next few months, I discussed the potential of this opportunity with the Baton Rouge firm with a few of my law partners with whom I was close, confidentially, and I explored with the Managing Partner of the Baton Rouge firm its level of interest in a larger group than just me and one or two younger attorneys. It so happens that the Baton Rouge firm had lost its partner in one of my areas of expertise and was looking to replace him, and the Managing Partner of the Baton Rouge firm (Scott) had worked for me one summer as a summer associate during his law school years. I had offered him a job after law school to work with our firm, but he declined because he was from Baton Rouge, which is only 90 miles from New Orleans, and wanted to live and practice in Baton Rouge. So, here he was years later the Managing Partner of a major Baton Rouge firm seeking to hire me.

After a lot of discussions over several months spearheaded by him and me, eight of us from my firm left it to join the New

Orleans office of the Baton Rouge firm. Four of us joined as equity partners. There was one major issue, though, that threatened to kill the deal – this firm had an age rule of 70, which I did not like at all since 70 was only four years away for me. That firm agreed to eliminate its age rule too, and the deal was sealed a few days later.

One of my claims to fame, as I tell my family, is that I had the age rules of two major law firms eliminated to accommodate me. Well, leaving a law firm after over 35 years was not easy at all, as I expected would be the situation, but I managed to do it successfully and to avoid any litigation with my former firm about it. In short, I left one law firm and joined another relatively seamlessly without any major turmoil, and I felt good about my move.

Almost 13 years later and counting, it has been good for me.

The name of my new firm is Breazeale, Sachse & Wilson ("BSW"). It turns out, as I learned after joining it, that Breazeale and Sachse were Jewish. I also learned soon after joining BSW how nice everyone there was as people and as partners. When I was asked about the adjustment for me at age 66 of the move to BSW, my standard reply was that the biggest adjustment for me was "to accept graciously how nice everyone is compared to my former firm." As mentioned, there were a lot of unpleasant politics at my former firm ever since I joined it 36 years earlier, but I stayed there because the money was good. At BSW, the money has been good too and everyone has remained so nice.

All Good Years Too: Ages 70-79

At age 70 I was asked to serve on the Management Committee ("MC") of BSW. I did for four years until age 74. That was stressful for me, being the only member of the MC from New Orleans and representing all of us in New Orleans. The MC meetings were weekly. Dealing with compensation issues for the entire law firm, including the New Orleans office, was particularly stressful. But I did get to know better the other MC partners in Baton Rouge, and the other partners there, and I enjoyed the experience.

After serving on the MC for four years, one of the younger partners in New Orleans (Peter) told me privately that he would like the opportunity to serve on the MC. I told him he would not like it at all, and why he wouldn't, but he wanted it. After some reflection I told him that I would withdraw from it and would support him for it so he could serve. At the election of the MC members he was elected easily. He has done a good job serving and has complained about its burdens to me privately. We remain close still.

BSW is well managed, makes good money, and remains such a nice place to work. Two of the partners are the son and grandson of former Governors of Louisiana. All of the partners are excellent attorneys, and BSW has a strong reputation in the State. I am fortunate to still work there.

That next year in March 2020 the pandemic started and lasted through most of 2021. That's practically two years; Katrina had only lasted for four months from late August until the end of 2005. The pandemic was difficult for us because, among other things, the elderly were especially vulnerable to death if they got the virus (first called Coronavirus, as if it were the beer Corona's virus, and later COVID). My health was still good, and I figured that even if I got it I would probably survive. I was more concerned that Sherrie might get it and die; she is younger by five years but possibly not as healthy.

The recovery from Katrina and from the pandemic and the duration of each were very different. Katrina lasted for four high stress months for us, plus longer until we had finished mourning over it. Let's say a year. After that year, everything was back to normal for New Orleans (to the extent New Orleans is ever normal). The pandemic lasted for most of two years, 2020 and 2021, and lingered for another year, 2022, or thereabouts. That's three years of dealing with the pandemic. I would say that by 2023 forward, life had returned to the full normal. But those three years of dealing with the pandemic were difficult, and perhaps scars from it remain.

Hell, in 2020 when I was 75 we also had to deal with two bad hurricanes in New Orleans. For one we moved to Sherrie's sister's house for about 4-5 days because we lost electricity in ours. Our food when we returned had all spoiled. That cleanup was not fun, which we did ourselves.

In 2021, Hurricane Ida came through New Orleans, and we evacuated to Allison's home in Atlanta and stayed for two weeks until our electricity was restored. That was not fun either.

I'm not sure what the scars from the pandemic are, or even if there are any. I do know that I became older during those years. I also know that I learned to adjust to having less of a social life due to the pandemic, and have remained less social with friends and others. I suppose the combination of the pandemic and the restrictions imposed on us from it, and my aging during it, have together led me to be more introspective and less social. I have found my friends are too.

In 2024, our son Dustin has gotten married, and we're

excited for him and her. He's our last child to get married. That's good!! They have been living in New Orleans the last four years, and we of course enjoy them whenever we're with them.

In June 2022, Sherrie and I were married for 50 years. Just upon returning to New Orleans from a short vacation, my family surprised us for it. My daughters and their families lived in Austin, Atlanta, and Kansas City, and they all came in town to celebrate us. Dustin already lived here. That was really special!! Two nights and two days we celebrated us. They made up and sang songs about us. They wrote poems for us. They had eyeglasses with "50" on them made, and handkerchiefs too. The Banner reading "Happy 50th Anniversary" for the two special dinners now hangs above our bed.

There is not too much more to tell about this period. I came to realize somewhere during my 70's that I had become old. Such a derogatory word in our society, it seems! There is even a term for when elderly people are treated unfairly: Age discrimination. While I personally have not experienced any age discrimination, I'm aware that others may be treating me differently due to my age. Notwithstanding, I have come to embrace my elderly status and to let others know my brain still works well. 😊

One thing that has endured for me for over 50 years and has led to my longevity as a hard-working attorney is all of the different and interesting matters, in a number of very different practice areas of the law, I have handled over the years. I've mentioned some of the interesting matters I worked on at Covington and before then during my Judicial Clerkship. Some of the others I worked on after returning to New Orleans include matters in the following areas of the practice of law: (a) Class Actions; (b) Securities fraud claims under both Federal and State law; (c) Trademark litigation; (d) Chapter 11 Reorganizations and Bankruptcy more generally; (e) Tax work, including both advising others and litigation matters; (f) Product liability litigation; (g) Mergers and acquisitions, including being the lead attorney in a number of major transactions; and (h) Commercial litigation of all types, including Admiralty litigation.

Switching my focus from one type of case (or matter) to another involved a lot of work. For example, when I was asked to defend a major high profile trademark case in New Orleans, the first thing I did was to gather and read about 20 different trademark cases over a weekend to get a "better feel" for the situation at hand. I also obtained help on the matter from one of the junior partners who had done some work in the area. After we lost the case in the trial court, we appealed and obtained a reversal. The local newspaper was covering the matter, and the clients wanted me to speak freely to the press on their behalf. Being quoted in the newspaper was fun of course, but it also raised my profile as an attorney in the City.

Another high profile case involved a local museum in New Orleans which was located in a beautiful residential area of the City. The museum had started hosting large late-night parties at its beautiful venue which were disturbing the neighbors. They sued, with me as their attorney, and we won in the trial court, lost in the intermediate appellate court, but then won in the Louisiana Supreme Court unanimously. The clients included a major movie and television star actor and a former basketball great in the NBA. The press reported on the case extensively and quoted from our court filings. That too raised my profile in the City.

Another matter involved the manager of the Ziggy Marley band. Ziggy is the son of Bob Marley (the well-known Reggae musician) and the manager's stage name was "Sky High."

Seriously!! He was standing outside the well-known venue "House of Blues" in the French Quarter of New Orleans when the police beat him up badly for reasons which were never fully explained to me, other than he may have said something to the police. I recall meeting with "Sky High" the next day; he was badly bruised from the encounter. We sued the City, and that case settled prior to trial.

Bottom line, I've always been just a hard-working person like most of us but have been fortunate and blessed to have worked on so many different and varying matters over the decades which have kept me engaged practicing law.

My brother Carl, who is now 86 and is a doctor, still goes to the office every day and sees patients. Malcolm, who is 82 and is a Ph.D. engineer, still works too. I enjoy my daily weekday routine and am not working a grueling schedule as I used to do. I can't, but I can still be productive and that feels good for me. As I tell others, in the late afternoons my light bulb starts to dim. But getting paychecks still is fun; it validates that I bring value to my law firm. Being at the office with younger, highly intelligent people is fun too. It provides me with a social life daily, and getting some work done for clients and accomplishing something worthwhile for them makes me feel good too.

Sherrie & Alan at Brittany's wedding

Family photo - Brittany & Joe's wedding

CONCLUSION

Thus my journey continues forward. Life is a journey for all of us. I want my life to stay that way.

One of my children has described this book as being about the value of drive, ambition, hard work, being competitive, winning (and losing), and success. I agree to an extent. It's also about having "fun" (however one defines that word) through it all, including laughing and loving and whatever else one finds enjoyable. Writing this book has been enjoyable for me. It's also my legacy to my children and their families and however I can help them to be all they can be and the best versions of themselves.Family photo - Brittany & Joe's wedding